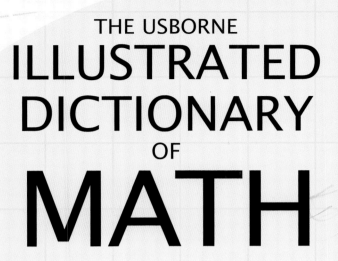

THE USBORNE
ILLUSTRATED
DICTIONARY
OF
MATH

Tori Large

Designed and illustrated by Adam Constantine

Edited by Kirsteen Rogers

Cover design: Russell Punter

Consultants:
Paul Metcalf
(Education Consultant and Principal Moderator)

Wendy Troy
(Goldsmith's College, London)

Frances C. Jamieson

Americanization: Carrie Seay

WHAT IS MATH?

Math, or mathematics, is the study of the relationship between size, shape and quantity, using numbers and symbols. In this book, math is divided into four sections. The areas covered by these sections are explained below.

Numbers

Introduces many different types of numbers, showing how they are the building blocks of mathematical calculations as well as being essential tools in everyday life.

Shape, space and measures

Covers the properties and measurements of the many different shapes and solids around us. Also includes everyday units of measurement such as length, mass and capacity.

Algebra

Algebra is the branch of math that uses letters and symbols to represent numbers and express the relationships between them. This section covers the various methods of simplifying and solving algebraic equations, including drawing and interpreting graphs.

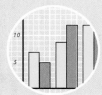

Handling data

Explains the different ways of collecting and analyzing information, and how the resulting data can be displayed in graphs, charts and tables.

CONTENTS

INTERNET LINKS

For each topic in this book, we have chosen some of the most interesting and exciting websites where you can find out more about the subject, or practice using what you have learned. To visit the sites, go to the Usborne Quicklinks Website at **www.usborne-quicklinks.com** and type the keywords "math dictionary." There you will find links to click on to take you to all the sites.

Here are some of the things you can do on the websites we recommend:

- find math puzzles, quizzes and games to test your skill and improve your performance

- take a visual tour of the universe from outer space to the innermost parts of an atom, using math terms to express the vast distance traveled

- control a car by altering the magnitude and direction of vectors

- check your progress with online worksheets and have your answers checked in an instant

- learn how to use mental math tricks to perform difficult calculations in your head

- find further examples and explanations to help you explore deeper into a topic area

How to access the websites
For links to the websites recommended for each topic in this book, go to the Usborne Quicklinks Website at **www.usborne-quicklinks.com** and enter the keywords "math dictionary," then follow the instructions you find there.

Internet safety
When using the Internet, please make sure you follow these guidelines:

- Children should ask their parent's or guardian's permission before they connect to the Internet.

- If you write a message in a website guest book or on a website message board, do not include any personal information such as your full name, address or telephone number, and ask an adult before you give your email address.

- If a website asks you to log in or register by typing your name or email address, ask permission of an adult first.

- If you receive an email from someone you don't know, tell an adult and do not reply to the email.

- Never arrange to meet anyone you have talked to on the Internet.

Site availability
The links in Usborne Quicklinks are regularly reviewed and updated, but occasionally you may get a message saying that a site is unavailable. This might be temporary, so try again later, or even the next day. If any of the sites close down, we will, if possible, replace them with suitable alternatives, so you will always find an up-to-date list of sites in Usborne Quicklinks.

Using the Internet

Most of the websites described in this book can be accessed with a standard home computer and a web browser (the software that enables you to display information from the Internet).

Extras

Some websites need additional free programs, called plug-ins, to play sounds, or to show videos, animations or 3-D images. If you go to a site and you do not have the necessary plug-in, a message saying so will come up on the screen. There is usually a button on the site that you can click on to download the plug-in. Alternatively, go to **www.usborne-quicklinks.com** and click on "Net Help." There you can find links to download plug-ins. Here is a list of plug-ins that you might need:

RealOne™ Player – lets you play video and hear sound files

QuickTime – enables you to view video clips

Flash™ – lets you play animations

Shockwave® – lets you play animations and interactive programs

Help

For general help and advice on using the Internet, go to Usborne Quicklinks at **www.usborne-quicklinks.com** and click on "Net Help." To find out more about how to use your web browser, click on "Help" at the top of the browser, and then choose "Contents and Index." You'll find a huge searchable dictionary containing tips on how to find your way easily around the Internet.

Computer viruses

A computer virus is a program that can seriously damage your computer. A virus can get into your computer when you download programs from the Internet, or in an attachment (an extra file) that arrives with an email. We strongly recommend that you buy anti-virus software to protect your computer and that you update the software regularly. For more information about viruses, go to Usborne Quicklinks and click on "Net Help."

Note for parents and guardians

The websites described in Usborne Quicklinks are regularly reviewed and the links are updated. However, the content of a website may change at any time and Usborne Publishing is not responsible for the content of any website other than its own.

We recommend that children are supervised while on the Internet, that they do not use Internet chat rooms, and that you use Internet filtering software to block unsuitable material. Please ensure that your children read and follow the safety guidelines on these pages.

For more information, see the "Net Help" area on the Usborne Quicklinks Website.

> **Computer not essential**
> If you don't have access to the Internet, don't worry. This book is a complete, self-contained reference book on its own.

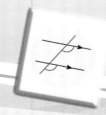

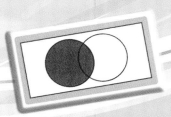

NUMBERS

Numbers are the basic building blocks of mathematics. Some numbers share common properties and can be grouped together in sets.

Digit
Any of the ten (Hindu-Arabic) numbers: 0, 1, 2, 3, 4, 5, 6, 7, 8, 9.

Number system
A way of using numbers to help us with counting. The **base ten** number system, for example, has ten digits (0, 1, 2, 3, 4, 5, 6, 7, 8, 9) that can be arranged to represent larger numbers. This number system is used by many people today. It is thought that it developed because people used their ten fingers and ten toes to help them count. The **binary** or **base two** number system is used by computers and it uses only two digits: 0 and 1.

Integers
The name for the set of **positive** and **negative numbers**, together with zero.
e.g. ⁻11, ⁻4, 0, 3, 8, 12

Integers do not include fractions*, decimals* or mixed numbers*, so $\frac{1}{2}$, 0.32, $6\frac{5}{8}$ are not integers.

Integers   Not integers

Natural or counting numbers
The positive **integers** we use for counting.
e.g. 1, 2, 3, 4
Natural numbers can be added, subtracted, multiplied and divided (see pages 14–15).

Consecutive numbers
Numbers that are next to each other.
e.g. 4, 5, 6, 7, 8...

Place value
The value of a **digit**, relating to its position. For example, the figures 12, 205 and 2,600 all contain the digit 2, but the place value of 2 is different in each of them. In the number 12, the 2 stands for 2 units. In 205, the 2 stands for 2 hundreds, while in 2,600 the 2 stands for 2 thousands. The value of a digit is increased by a power* of ten for each successive place to the left, and decreased by a power of ten for each successive place to the right.

Thousands	Hundreds	Tens	Units		Tenths	Hundredths
0	2	0	5	•	0	0

Decimal point*

The diagram above shows how the number 205 means 2 hundreds, 0 tens and 5 units. Any zeros in front of the first significant figure* (here, the 2), can be ignored.

* **Decimal, Decimal point** 19; **Fraction** 17; **Mixed numbers** 18; **Power** 21; **Remainder** 15; **Significant figure** 9.

Positive number

Any number above zero.

e.g. $^+1$, $^+6.5$, $^+327$

Positive numbers can be written with a plus sign (+) in front of the number, but are usually written without any sign. Any number without a sign in front of it is assumed to be positive.

*One of the common ways in which both **positive** and **negative** numbers are used in everyday life is in measuring temperature. If the temperature falls below 0°C or 0°F, it is measured using negative numbers.*

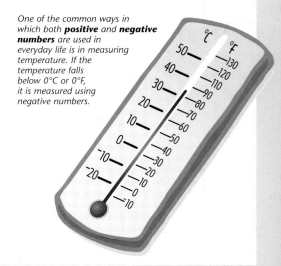

Negative number

Any number below zero.

e.g. $^-3$, $^-21.8$, $^-40$

Negative numbers are always written with a minus sign (−) in front of the number. To avoid confusion with subtraction, the minus sign can be placed in a raised position, e.g. $^-3$.

Use the +/− key on your calculator to convert a positive number to a negative number.

Directed numbers

All **positive** and **negative numbers**. These can be represented on a **number line**, like the one pictured below. Directed numbers are so called because it is important to take into account the direction they are measured from zero.

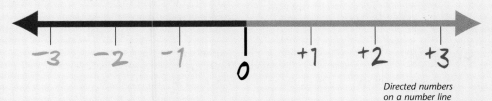

Directed numbers on a number line

Even number

Any **integer** that can be divided by 2 without leaving a remainder*.

e.g. $^-2$, 2, 4, 6

Any integer that ends with 0, 2, 4, 6 or 8 is an even number. 114, 2748 and 357 196 are all even numbers.

Odd number

Any **integer** that cannot be divided by 2 without leaving a remainder*.

e.g. $^-1$, 1, 3, 5

Any integer that ends with 1, 3, 5, 7 or 9 is an odd number. 47, 579 and 82 603 are all odd numbers.

Prime number

A number that can only be divided by 1 and itself. The first ten prime numbers are:

2 3 5 7 11 13 17 19 23 29

There is an infinite number of prime numbers: the list never ends.

It is important to remember that:

• 1 is not considered to be a prime number.
• 2 is the only **even** prime number.

Composite number

Any number that is not a **prime number**.

e.g. 6, 9, 20, 27

Internet links For links to useful websites on **numbers**, go to *www.usborne-quicklinks.com*

Square number

A positive number* that is the result of multiplying an integer by itself. (This is called **squaring** the number.)

e.g. $4 \times 4 = \mathbf{16}$
$7 \times 7 = \mathbf{49}$
$^-5 \times {}^-5 = \mathbf{25}$

The first ten square numbers are:

1 4 9 16 25 36 49 64 81 100

The list of square numbers is infinite. They are called square numbers because they can be represented by units in a square.

The square number 16 can be represented by a square pattern of dots measuring 4 × 4.

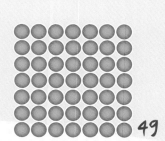

The square number 49 can be represented by a square pattern of dots measuring 7 × 7.

Triangular number

A positive number* that is the sum* of consecutive integers.

e.g.
$1 = \mathbf{1}$
$1 + 2 = \mathbf{3}$
$1 + 2 + 3 = \mathbf{6}$
$1 + 2 + 3 + 4 = \mathbf{10}$

These numbers can be represented by units in a triangle. Each new triangle is formed by adding another row of dots to the previous triangle.

The first ten triangular numbers are:

1 3 6 10 15 21 28 36 45 55

The list of triangular numbers is infinite.

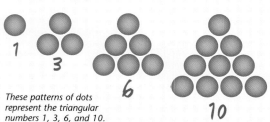

These patterns of dots represent the triangular numbers 1, 3, 6, and 10.

Cube number

A positive number* that is the result of multiplying an integer by itself, then multiplying by itself again. (This is called **cubing** the number.)

e.g. $4 \times 4 \times 4 = \mathbf{64}$

The first ten cube numbers are:

1 8 27 64 125 216 343 512 729 1000

The list of cube numbers is infinite. They are called cube numbers because they can be represented by units in a cube.

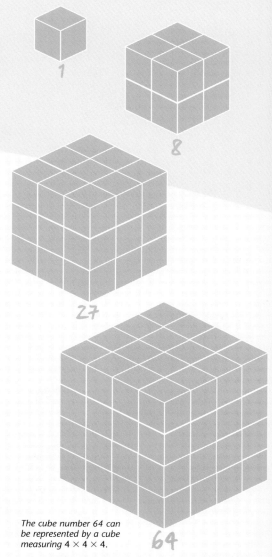

The cube number 64 can be represented by a cube measuring 4 × 4 × 4.

*Decimal, Decimal place 19; Denominator 17; Digit 6; Fraction 17; Integer 6; Negative number 7; Numerator 17; Pi 66; Place value 6; Positive number 7; Recurring decimal 19; Rounding 16; Set 12; Square root 11; Sum 14 (Addition); Terminating decimal 19.

Palindrome

A number that reads the same from right to left as it does from left to right, e.g. 23 432.

Pandigital number

A number that contains each of the digits 0, 1, 2, 3, 4, 5, 6, 7, 8 and 9 only once, e.g. 2 918 653 470.

Rational number

Any number that can be written as a fraction*, where the numerator* and denominator* are integers*. The integers can be positive* or negative*. Any terminating decimal*, such as 50.856, and any recurring decimal*, such as $0.\overline{3}$, can be written as a rational number.

e.g. $50.856 = \dfrac{50\,856}{1000}$ $\quad 0.\overline{3} = \dfrac{3}{9} = \dfrac{1}{3}$

Irrational number

A number that is not **rational** and so cannot be written exactly as a fraction* or a decimal*. In an irrational number, the number of decimal places* is infinite and there is no recurring pattern within the number. Pi* (π) is an irrational number that begins 3.141 592 653...

Real numbers

The set* of all **rational** and **irrational numbers**.

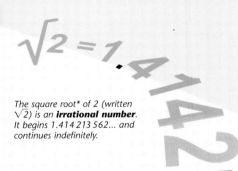

The square root of 2 (written $\sqrt{2}$) is an **irrational number**. It begins 1.414 213 562... and continues indefinitely.*

Significant figure

The digit* in a number that indicates its size to a certain degree of accuracy. The first and most significant figure is the first non-zero digit in a number, as this has the highest value. For example, in the number 4,209 the first significant figure is 4 because it tells us that the number is four thousand and something. The 9, although a larger digit, only represents nine units and is therefore the least significant figure here. After the first significant figure, any zero also counts as a significant figure.

Answers to calculations are often rounded* to a specified number of significant figures (**sig. fig.** or **s.f.**), for example 1 s.f., 2 s.f. or 3 s.f.. The normal rules for rounding* apply. (If the number to be rounded is to the left of a 5 or above, it is always rounded up.)

For example, if 328,000 were written to 2 s.f., we would write down the 3, and then decide whether the 2 should be rounded up or not. As the next figure, 8, is closer to 10 than to 0, the 2 is rounded up, making the answer 330,000.

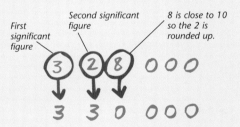

The same applies to decimal numbers. For example, the first significant figure in 0.000 459 1 is 4. The zeros are important as they hold the place value* but they do not count as significant figures. If this number were written to 2 s.f. it would be 0.000 46.

First significant figure   *Second significant figure*   *9 is close to 10 so the 5 is rounded up.*

The zeros do not count as significant figures.

0.000 ④⑤⑨1

0.000 4 6

Sequences

A list of numbers that follow a particular pattern or rule is called a **sequence**. Each number or shape in a sequence is called a **term** of the sequence. If the rule is not given, it can usually be worked out from the first few numbers in the sequence.

Linear sequence

A sequence that increases or decreases by a constant*. The formula* $2n - 1$ gives the sequence:

$$1, 3, 5, 7, 9, 11...$$

which goes up in 2s.

This is because:

$$(2 \times 1) - 1 = 1$$
$$(2 \times 2) - 1 = 3$$
$$(2 \times 3) - 1 = 5... \text{ and so on.}$$

Quadratic sequence

A sequence that includes a squared number. The formula* $n^2 + 1$ gives the sequence:

$$2, 5, 10, 17, 26...$$

This is because:

$$1^2 + 1 = 2$$
$$2^2 + 1 = 5$$
$$3^2 + 1 = 10... \text{ and so on.}$$

In some cases, a rule can be expressed as a formula for a typical member of the sequence. In the example above, to find the 7th number in the sequence, apply the rule $n^2 + 1$ to the number 7:

$$7^2 + 1 = 49 + 1 = 50$$

The value of any number in this sequence can be found by applying the rule in this way.

Fibonacci sequence

The sequence:

$$1, 1, 2, 3, 5, 8, 13...$$

Each number (from the third number onwards) is calculated by adding together the previous two numbers. For example, the next number in the sequence is calculated by adding together 8 and 13, to give 21.

Any sequence that follows this rule can be described as a Fibonacci sequence.

e.g. $7, 10, 17, 27...$

The Fibonacci sequence, identified by Leonardo Fibonacci in 1202, often appears in nature.

The Fibonacci sequence can be seen in the spiral of a shell. You can recreate this spiral by drawing a series of squares with side lengths that follow the Fibonacci sequence (1, 1, 2, 3, 5 ...).

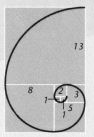 

Starting with the first box, draw a curve from the top right hand corner to the opposite corner, and continue through the rest of the squares.

The result is a spiral like that seen on this shell.

Chinese or Pascal's triangle

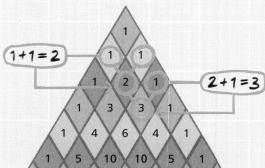

The number at the point of **Pascal's triangle** is 1 and each row starts and ends with 1. Each of the other numbers in the triangle is the result of adding together the two numbers above it, such as $3 + 3 = 6$. The triangle was used as early as 1300 in China.

It was later named after the French mathematician Blaise Pascal (1623–62), who brought it to the attention of Western mathematicians. The triangular pattern is now often used in determining probability*.

** **Constant** 75; **Formula** 75; **Negative number, Positive number, Prime number** 7; **Probability** 112; **Set** 12; **Sum** 14 (**Addition**).*

Multiples

A **multiple** of a number is the result of multiplying that number with a whole number.
e.g. $3 \times 2 = 6$ $3 \times 4 = 12$ $3 \times 6 = 18$
So, 6, 12 and 18 are all multiples of 3.

Common multiple

A number that is a multiple of two or more other numbers.
e.g.   Multiples of 2 include 2, 4, 6, 8, 10, 12
       Multiples of 3 include 3, 6, 9, 12, 15
So the common multiples of 2 and 3 from the sets* above are 6 and 12.

The **lowest** or **least common multiple (LCM)** of two or more numbers is the smallest number that is a multiple of each. The least common multiple of 2 and 3 is 6.

Factors

A **factor** of a number is any whole number that divides into it exactly. While a prime number* has only two factors (1 and itself), other numbers can have many factors. For example, the factors of 12 are 1, 2, 3, 4, 6 and 12. Any whole number can be written as a product of its factors.
e.g. $12 = 2 \times 6$ $12 = 3 \times 4$

Common factor

A number that divides exactly into two or more other numbers.
e.g.   Factors of 15 are 1, 3, 5, 15
       Factors of 40 are 1, 2, 4, 5, 8, 10, 20, 40
The common factors of 15 and 40 are 1 and 5.

The **greatest common factor (GCF)** of two or more numbers is the largest number that is a factor of each. The greatest common factor of 15 and 40 is 5.

Prime factor

A **factor** that is also a prime number*. The factors of 12 are 1, 2, 3, 4, 6 and 12. Of these numbers, 1, 2 and 3 are prime factors.

Perfect number

A number that is the sum* of its **factors** (excluding itself), e.g. $6 = 1 + 2 + 3$.

Roots

Square root

A **factor** of a number that can be squared (multiplied by itself) to equal that number.

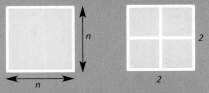

The square root of a square of area n^2 is n (where n is the length of a side).

For example, $2 \times 2 = 4$, so 2 is the square root of 4.

Every positive number* has two square roots: a positive one and a negative one. (If you multiply $^{-}4 \times ^{-}4$, the answer is still 16.)

A square root is written with the symbol $\sqrt{}$. $\sqrt{9}$ means the positive square root of 9, and $^{-}\sqrt{9}$ means the negative square root of 9. The positive and negative square roots of 9 are written as $\pm\sqrt{9}$.

Use the square root key on your calculator to find the square root of a number.

Cube root

A **factor** of a number that can be cubed (multiplied by itself, then by itself again) to equal that number.

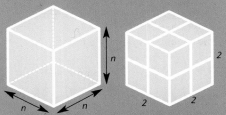

The cube root of a cube of volume n^3 is n (where n is the length of a side).

For example, $2 \times 2 \times 2 = 8$, so 2 is the cube root of 8.

Any positive or negative number* has only one cube root. A cube root is written with the symbol $\sqrt[3]{}$.

Use the cube root key on your calculator to find the cube root of a number.

SETS

A **set** is a group of objects that have something in common or follow a rule. Every object in a set is unique: the same object cannot be included in the set more than once. Sets can be used to show the relationship between different groups of objects.

Braces can be used to indicate that the objects written between them belong to a set.

Set notation

The objects belonging to a set are placed between **braces**, and separated from each other with commas.

e.g.   {a, e, i, o, u}

This method is called **roster notation**.

The order in which objects are listed in a set is not important.

e.g.   {a, e, i, o, u} = {u, o, a, e, i} and so on.

It is not necessary to list every object in the set. Instead, the rule that the objects follow can be given in the braces:

e.g.   {vowels}

This is particularly useful when handling very large sets.

e.g.   {numbers from 1 to 1000}

Sets are often represented by a single letter.

e.g.   A = {even numbers}

Some commonly used sets are always represented by a particular letter. These are:

$\mathbb{Z}$ = the set of integers*
$\mathbb{N}$ = the set of natural numbers*
$\mathbb{Q}$ = the set of rational numbers*
$\mathbb{R}$ = the set of real numbers*

Element or member

An object that belongs to a set. The symbol $\in$ means "is an element of" or "is a member of." The symbol $\notin$ means "is not an element of" or "is not a member of." For example, 1 is an element of the set $\mathbb{N} = \{1, 2, 3, 4, 5 ...\}$. This can also be written as $1 \in \mathbb{N}$. The number $^-1$ is not an element of this set, so this relationship can be written as $^-1 \notin \mathbb{N}$.

Universal set

The set that contains all other sets. For example, if set C = {consonants}, the universal set is the alphabet. The universal set is represented by the symbol $\mathscr{E}$. e.g. $\mathscr{E}$ = {alphabet}

Finite set

A set that contains a limited number of **elements**. For example, set A is the set of odd numbers* between 0 and 6:

A = {1, 3, 5}

A is a finite set, because $n(A) = 3$ (where n is the number of elements in a set).

Infinite set

A set that contains an unlimited number of **elements**. For example, the set of odd numbers* is an infinite set: it never ends. You can indicate that a set is infinite by writing down the first few elements, followed by a series of dots.

e.g.   B = {1, 3, 5, 7 ...}

B is an infinite set, because $n(B) = \infty$ (where n is the number of elements in a set and the symbol ∞ represents infinity).

Empty set or null set

A set that contains no **elements**. For example, the set X = {days of the week starting with a "J"} is an empty set. An empty set is written as { }, or represented by the symbol $\varnothing$, so this example can also be written X = { } or X = $\varnothing$.

Subset

A set that also belongs to another set. For example, if set A = {consonants} and set B = {t, r, y}, B is said to be a subset of A. The symbol $\subset$ means "is a subset of," so this relationship can be written as B $\subset$ A. If set C = {a, e, i}, it is not a subset of A. The symbol $\not\subset$ means "is not a subset of," so this relationship can be written as C $\not\subset$ A.

*Integers, Natural numbers 6; Odd number, Prime number 7; Rational number, Real numbers 9.

Comparing sets

The relationship between two or more sets can be studied by looking at the **elements** of each set and deciding whether they share any common elements.

Complement of a set
The set of all **elements** that are not included in a particular set. For example, if A contains all prime numbers*, A′ contains all numbers that are not prime. This is the same as saying:

$$A' = \mathscr{E} - A$$

since the universal set $\mathscr{E}$ contains all numbers. The complement of set A is written as A′.

Union of sets
The **elements** of two or more sets together. This is represented by the symbol ∪ (called the **cup**). For example, if set A = {2, 4, 6} and set B = {1, 3, 5, 6}:

$$A \cup B = \{1, 2, 3, 4, 5, 6\}$$

Intersection of sets
The **elements** that appear in two or more sets. The intersection is represented by the symbol ∩ (called the **cap**). For example, if set A = {2, 4, 6} and set B = {1, 2, 3, 4, 5}:

$$A \cap B = \{2, 4\}$$

Venn diagrams

A **Venn diagram** shows the relationship between sets. In a Venn diagram, a set is usually represented by a circle, and the **universal set** by a rectangle. **Elements** of a set are often represented by points in the circle. Each part of the diagram is labeled and the parts being considered are shaded.

A Venn diagram

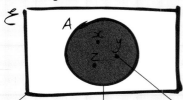

The rectangle represents the universal set.

This circle represents set A which is a subset of the universal set.

The points represent the elements of set A.

Venn diagrams of some common set relationships

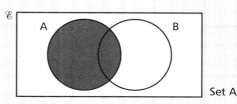
Set A

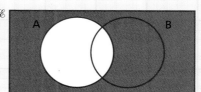
A′

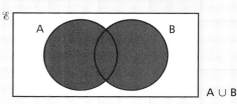
A ∪ B

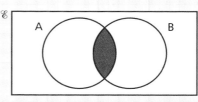
A ∩ B

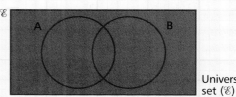
Universal set ($\mathscr{E}$)

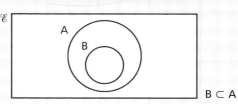
B ⊂ A

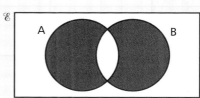
(A ∪ B) − A ∩ B

ARITHMETIC

Arithmetic is the ability to use numbers. The four basic operations used in calculations are **addition**, **subtraction**, **multiplication** and **division**.

Addition

Use the addition key on your calculator to perform addition.

The mathematical operation to find the **sum** of two numbers. It can be thought of as increasing one given number by another. Addition is usually written $a + b$.

e.g.　$6 + 3 = 9$

Addition is the opposite, or **inverse**, operation to **subtraction**, and it obeys the **associative** and **commutative laws**.

Subtraction

Use the subtraction key on your calculator to perform subtraction.

The mathematical operation in which the **difference** between two numbers is found. It can be thought of as reducing one number by another. Subtraction is usually written $a - b$.

e.g.　$10 - 6 = 4$

Subtraction is the opposite, or **inverse**, operation to **addition**. It does not obey the **associative** and **commutative laws**.

Multiplication

Use the multiplication key on your calculator to perform multiplication.

The mathematical operation in which two numbers are combined together to give a **product**.

e.g.　$6 \times 8 = 48$

As in the example above, multiplication is often written $a \times b$, but it can also be written $a.b$ or (if quantities are represented by symbols) ab.

Multiplication can be thought of as repeated addition.

e.g.　$3 \times 4 = (4 + 4 + 4)$ or $(3 + 3 + 3 + 3) = 12$

Multiplication is the opposite, or **inverse**, of **division**, and it obeys the **associative** and **commutative laws**.

Long multiplication

A method of multiplying large numbers without a calculator. Long multiplication is done in stages. It relies on the fact that any number can be broken down into the hundreds, tens and units, etc., that it contains.

e.g.　$143 = (1 \times 100) + (4 \times 10) + (3 \times 1)$

So, multiplying one number by another is the same as multiplying the first number by the hundreds, tens and units, etc., that make up the second number, and adding the results together.

e.g.　736×143
$= (736 \times 100) + (736 \times 40) + (736 \times 3)$

The digit representing the largest value is usually multiplied first, followed by the next largest and so on, working from right to left.

One way to write out long multiplication is shown below. The explanation (written here in parentheses) is not usually shown.

$$
\begin{array}{r}
736 \\
\times\ 143 \\
\hline
73600 \quad \text{(736} \times \text{100)} \\
29440 \quad \text{(736} \times \text{40)} \\
2208 \quad \text{(736} \times \text{3)} \\
\hline
105248 \quad \text{(add the totals)}
\end{array}
$$

Division

Use the division key on your calculator to perform division.

The mathematical operation to find the result (the **quotient**) of dividing one number by another number.
e.g. $40 \div 8 = 5$

As in the example above, division is often written $a \div b$, but can also be written a/b or $\frac{a}{b}$.

For example, 40 divided by 8 can be written in the following ways:
$$40 \div 8 \quad 40/8 \quad \frac{40}{8}$$

Division can be thought of as repeated **subtraction**, answering the question "how many times can the second number be taken from the first?" For example, the number of times that 5 can be taken away from 40 is 8:
$$40 - 5 - 5 - 5 - 5 - 5 - 5 - 5 - 5 = 0$$

Division is the opposite, or **inverse**, of **multiplication**. It does not obey the **associative** and **commutative** laws.

Remainder
In **division**, the amount left over when one number does not divide exactly into the other. For example if 16 is divided by 3, it will go 5 times, but there is 1 left over: this is the remainder. Remainder is sometimes abbreviated to "rem." or "r".

Long division
A process by which large numbers are divided without the use of a calculator. To divide 5,996 by 22, try to divide 22 into each digit of the larger number in turn, starting from the left. Join any remainder (rem.) to the next digit to create a new number for division.

5 (thousands) $\div$ 22 = 0 rem. 5 (thousands)
59 (hundreds) $\div$ 22 = 2 rem. 15 (hundreds)
159 (tens) $\div$ 22 = 7 rem. 5 (tens)
56 (units) $\div$ 22 = 2 rem. 12 (units)

So, the answer is 2 (hundred), 7 (tens) and 2 (units), remainder 12 units, that is, 272 rem. 12.

The conventional way to write down this calculation is shown here, though you may see long division set out in other ways.

The answer is built up in stages, corresponding to each part of the calculation.

$$2 \quad 7 \quad 2 \quad rem \, 1 \, 2$$
$$22 \overline{)5 \quad 9 \quad 9 \quad 6}$$
$$-\;4 \quad 4 \downarrow$$
Take 44 (2 × 22) from 59 to find the remainder.
$$1 \quad 5 \quad 9$$
"Bring down" the 9 and join it to the remainder.
$$-\;1 \quad 5 \quad 4 \downarrow$$
Take 154 (7 × 22) from 159 to find the remainder.
$$5 \quad 6$$
"Bring down" the 6 and join it to the remainder.
$$-\;4 \quad 4$$
Take 44 (2 × 22) from 56 to find the remainder.
$$1 \quad 2$$
When there are no more numbers to bring down, write the final remainder over the bar to complete the answer.

Laws of arithmetic

Associative law
The rule which states that the grouping of numbers or terms and symbols in an expression does not affect the result. Both **addition** and **multiplication** follow this rule, whereas **subtraction** and **division** do not.

The **associative law of addition** states that $(a + b) + c = a + (b + c)$.
e.g. $(12 + 7) + 6 = 12 + (7 + 6)$

The **associative law of multiplication** states that $(a \times b) \times c = a \times (b \times c)$.
e.g. $(5 \times 2) \times 4 = 5 \times (2 \times 4)$

Commutative law
The rule which states that the order in which numbers or terms and symbols in an expression are combined does not affect the result. Both **addition** and **multiplication** follow this rule.

The **commutative law of addition** states that $a + b = b + a$.
e.g. $6 + 3 = 3 + 6$

The **commutative law of multiplication** states that $a \times b = b \times a$.
e.g. $5 \times 3 = 3 \times 5$

Internet links For links to useful websites on **arithmetic**, go to www.usborne-quicklinks.com

Mixed operations

Calculations involving more than one type of operation. There are certain rules to follow when working with mixed operations.

If only addition* and subtraction* are involved in the calculation, the order in which they are done does not matter. However, it is important to remember that the + or − sign only applies to the number directly following it.

e.g. $\qquad$ $7 - 5 + 10$
is the same as $\qquad$ $7 + 10 - 5$
$\qquad$ or $\qquad$ $^-5 + 7 + 10$

If any other combination of operations is involved, the **PEMDAS** guidelines apply.

PEMDAS

The order in which operations should be performed in an expression involving mixed operations. PEMDAS stands for **P**arentheses, **E**xponents* (values raised to a power*), **M**ultiplication*, **D**ivision*, **A**ddition* and **S**ubtraction*. (An easy way to remember the order is **P**lease **E**xcuse **M**y **D**ear **A**unt **S**ally.)

For example, to find the answer to the sum $6 + 40 \div 20 \times (3 + 1)^2 - 3$:

Work out any grouping symbols, such as Parentheses:

$\qquad$ $6 + 40 \div 20 \times (3 + 1)^2 - 3$

Work out the Exponents:

$\qquad$ $6 + 40 \div 20 \times (4)^2 - 3$

Work out the Multiplication:

$\qquad$ $6 + 2 \times 16 - 3$

Work out the Division:

$\qquad$ $6 + 40 \div 20 \times 16 - 3$

Work out the Addition:

$\qquad$ $6 + 32 - 3$

Work out the Subtraction:

$\qquad$ $38 - 3$

So, the answer is 35.

Rounding

The process of approximating a figure by reducing the number of significant figures* or decimal places* is called **rounding**. The amount of approximation depends on the degree of accuracy required.

Numbers can be rounded to the nearest integer*, ten, hundred, or so on. Decimals* are often rounded to one or more decimal places. The way a number is rounded often depends on what is being measured. For example, a person's height is usually rounded to the nearest inch, whereas the population of a country may be rounded to the nearest hundred thousand people.

To round a number

Find the place in the number where the rounding is to be done and look at the digit to the right:
- If this is 5 or greater, increase the digit being rounded by 1.
- If it is 4 or less, the digit for rounding stays the same.

For example, 276 rounded to the nearest 10 would be 280, as 6 is closer to 10 than to 0, and so 276 is closer to 280 than 270. The number 4,872 rounded to the nearest 10 would be 4,870, and to the nearest 100 would be 4,900.

Upper bound

The highest value that would be rounded down to a number. For example, if the number of beans in a jar is given as 550 to the nearest ten beans, the true number will be in the range 545 to 554 beans. The value 554 is the upper bound.

Lower bound

The lowest value that would be rounded up to a number. For example, if the number of beans in a jar is given as 550 to the nearest ten beans, the true number will be in the range 545 to 554 beans. The value 545 is the lower bound.

---

* **Addition** 14; **Decimal, Decimal place** 19; **Division** 15; **Index** 21; **Integer** 6; **Multiple** 11; **Multiplication** 15; **Power** 21; **Significant figure** 9; **Subtraction** 14.

FRACTIONS

When something is divided into equal parts, each part is called a **fraction**. A fraction can be expressed as one number written above another ($\frac{x}{y}$). The number on the bottom (y) is called the **denominator** and the number on the top (x) is called the **numerator**.

Use the fraction key on your scientific calculator to input fractions.

Numerator
The top part of a fraction. The **numerator** represents the number of parts being considered. For example, the picture on the right shows three out of four pieces, or $\frac{3}{4}$, of a whole orange, so the numerator is 3.

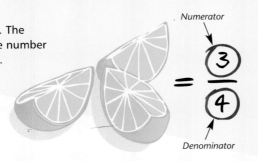

Numerator

$= \dfrac{3}{4}$

Denominator

Denominator
The bottom part of a fraction. The **denominator** represents the total number of equal parts. For example, the picture on the left shows three out of four pieces, or $\frac{3}{4}$, of a whole orange, so the denominator is 4.

Equivalent fractions
Fractions that refer to the same proportion of a whole, but are written in different ways.

The circles below have all been divided into a different number of equal parts. The section of the circle that is highlighted is described as three equivalent fractions:

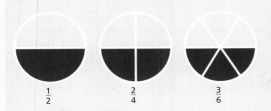

$\frac{1}{2}$ $\frac{2}{4}$ $\frac{3}{6}$

There is an infinite number of equivalent fractions. The way in which the fraction is expressed, or written, depends on how many parts the whole has been divided into. If it were to be divided into 20 equal parts, half of that would be expressed as $\frac{10}{20}$.

Equivalent fractions can be calculated by multiplying or dividing the numerator and denominator by the same number.

e.g. $\frac{1}{2} = \frac{1}{2} \times \frac{2}{2} = \frac{2}{4}$ $\frac{4}{8} = \frac{4}{8} \div \frac{4}{4} = \frac{1}{2}$

When the numerator and denominator are divided by the same number, the resulting fraction has a smaller numerator and denominator than the original. This is called **canceling** (or **simplifying**) the fraction. When the numerator and denominator of a fraction are canceled down to the smallest possible integers, the fraction is said to be in its **lowest possible terms**.

An easy way of comparing fractions is by expressing them with their **lowest common denominator**, i.e. the lowest multiple* of both denominators. For example, the lowest common denominator of $\frac{1}{2}$ and $\frac{2}{6}$ is 6, so the fractions can be expressed as $\frac{3}{6}$ and $\frac{2}{6}$.

Common or simple fraction

A fraction that has integers* for its numerator* and denominator*. This is the most frequently seen type of fraction.

e.g. $\frac{1}{2}$ $\frac{4}{3}$ $\frac{46}{19}$

Complex fraction

A fraction that has a numerator* or denominator*, or both, which is itself a fraction.

e.g.

$$\frac{2}{\frac{3}{5}} \qquad \frac{\frac{1}{4}}{2} \qquad \frac{\frac{1}{3}}{\frac{7}{8}}$$

Proper fraction

A fraction that is less than a whole unit. Any fraction with a numerator* that is lower than the denominator* is a proper fraction.

e.g. $\frac{1}{4}$ $\frac{4}{5}$ $\frac{40}{71}$

Improper or top heavy fraction

A fraction that is more than a whole unit. Any fraction with a numerator* that is higher than the denominator* is an improper fraction.

e.g. $\frac{3}{2}$ $\frac{7}{3}$ $\frac{412}{4}$

Mixed number

A number consisting of an integer* and a fraction. Mixed numbers can also be expressed as **improper fractions**. For example, $1\frac{1}{2}$ is a mixed number and can also be expressed as the improper fraction $\frac{3}{2}$.

Reciprocal

The reciprocal of a number is found by dividing 1 by that number. For example, the reciprocal of 3 is $\frac{1}{3}$.

To find a reciprocal of a fraction, simply invert the fraction (turn it upside down). For example, the reciprocal of $\frac{3}{4}$ is $\frac{4}{3}$ because:

$$1 \div \frac{3}{4} = \frac{1}{1} \div \frac{3}{4} = \frac{1}{1} \times \frac{4}{3} = \frac{4}{3}$$

 Use the reciprocal key on your scientific calculator to find the reciprocal of a number.

Fractions and percentages

Fractions can be expressed as a percentage*, that is, a number of parts in 100.
For example, 25% means $\frac{25}{100}$.

Any fraction can be turned into a percentage simply by multiplying the fraction by 100.

e.g. $\frac{1}{2} = (\frac{1}{2} \times 100)\% = 50\%$

$\frac{3}{4} = (\frac{3}{4} \times 100)\% = 75\%$

A percentage can be turned into a fraction by dividing it by 100 and canceling* it down to its lowest possible terms*.

e.g. $25\% = (\frac{25}{100}) = \frac{1}{4}$

Arithmetic with fractions

To add a fraction

Express each fraction in terms of the lowest common denominator* and add the numerators* together.

e.g. $\frac{2}{3} + \frac{1}{2} = \frac{4}{6} + \frac{3}{6} = \frac{7}{6} = 1\frac{1}{6}$

To subtract a fraction

Express each fraction in terms of the lowest common denominator* and subtract the numerators*.

e.g. $\frac{3}{4} - \frac{1}{3} = \frac{9}{12} - \frac{4}{12} = \frac{5}{12}$

To multiply a fraction

Multiply the numerators* together and then multiply the denominators* together.

e.g. $\frac{3}{4} \times \frac{1}{2} = \frac{3 \times 1}{4 \times 2} = \frac{3}{8}$

To multiply **mixed numbers**, first turn them into **improper fractions**.

To divide a fraction

Multiply the fraction by its **reciprocal**.

e.g. $\frac{1}{2} \div \frac{3}{8} = \frac{1}{2} \times \frac{3}{8} = \frac{1 \times 8}{2 \times 3} = \frac{8}{6} = 1\frac{2}{6} = 1\frac{1}{3}$

To divide **mixed numbers**, first turn them into **improper fractions**.

*Base ten 6 (Number system); Canceling 17 (Equivalent fractions); Denominator 17; Integers 6; Lowest common denominator 17 (Equivalent fractions); Lowest possible terms 17 (Equivalent fractions); Multiple 11; Numerator 17; Percentage 27; Pi 66; Place value 6; Power 21.

DECIMALS

The **decimal system** is a number system that uses base ten*.
A number written using the decimal number system is called
a **decimal**. Most commonly, this term refers to a number in
which any parts less than an integer* are written after the
decimal point, for example, 1.2 or 59.635 or 0.0091.

The diagram below shows the place value* represented by each digit in the decimal 6,539.023.

Thousands	Hundreds	Tens	Units		Tenths	Hundredths	Thousandths
6	5	3	9	.	0	2	3

Decimal point

Each successive place to the left is increased by one power* of ten. Each successive place to the
right is decreased by one power of ten.

Decimal place
The position of a number to the right of the
decimal point. The first position to the right of
the decimal point is the first decimal place, and
the next position is the second decimal place
and so on.

Decimal fraction
Any number less than 1 that is expressed as a
decimal. For example, 0.375 is a decimal fraction
that expresses:

$$0 + \frac{3}{10} + \frac{7}{100} + \frac{5}{1000}$$

Decimal fractions are also called just **decimals**.

Mixed decimal
A number that is made up of an integer and a
decimal fraction. For example, 15.76 is a mixed
decimal that expresses $15 + \frac{7}{10} + \frac{6}{100}$.

Finite decimal or terminating decimal
A **decimal** that has a fixed number of
decimal places.

e.g. $\frac{1}{2} = 0.5$ as a decimal

$\frac{17}{625} = 0.0272$ as a decimal

Note that these fractions have denominators*
which are a multiple* of 2 or 5. This is true of
all terminating decimals when they are written
as a fraction.

Decimal point
A dot used to separate units from tenths. It
may be placed centrally between the numbers
(e.g. 1·2) but is now more usually placed on
the line (e.g. 1.2). Some countries use a comma
in place of a dot (e.g. 1,2) to avoid confusion
with a dot that they use as a symbol for
multiplication.

Infinite or non-terminating decimal
A **decimal** that does not have a fixed number of
decimal places. There are two kinds of infinite
decimals: **non-repeating** and **recurring decimals**.

Non-repeating or non-periodic decimal
An **infinite decimal** in which the sequence of
digits after the **decimal point** is not repeated.
One example is the decimal form of Pi* (π),
which begins 3.141 592 653...

Recurring decimal
An **infinite decimal** in which the sequence of
digits after the **decimal point** repeats itself
infinitely (endlessly).

e.g. 3.333 333...
0.125 125 125...

Recurring decimals are written with lines over
the recurring figure or figures. So, the examples
above would be written as $3.\overline{3}$ and $0.\overline{125}$.

Arithmetic with decimals

To add or subtract a decimal

It is easier to add and subtract decimals* by writing the numbers in a column, with the decimal points* lined up.

e.g.   11.45 + 17 + 2.5 is written:

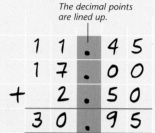

The decimal points are lined up.

As with addition of integers, start the sum at the right-hand side and work left.

e.g.   50.19 − 36.2 is written:

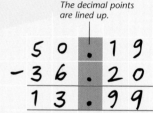

The decimal points are lined up.

As with subtraction of integers, start the sum at the right-hand side and work left.

To divide by a decimal

Ignore the decimal point* to give integers (ensuring that the resulting numbers are all increased to the same **power** of ten). Then divide the numbers: the result will be the same as if dividing decimals*.

e.g.   3.2 ÷ 0.4

$$\overset{\times\,10}{\frac{3.2}{0.4}} = \frac{32}{4} = 8$$

$\times\,10$

To multiply by a decimal

Ignore the decimal point* and multiply as integers. Then insert the decimal point so that the number of decimal places* (d.p.) is the same as the total number of decimal places in the numbers being multiplied.

e.g.   3.5 × 2.36
            (1 d.p.) (2 d.p.)

Use: 35 × 236

$$
\begin{array}{r}
35 \\
\times\ 236 \\
\hline
210 \\
1050 \\
7000 \\
\hline
8260 \\
\end{array}
$$

(35 × 6)
(35 × 30)
(35 × 200)
(add the totals)

So: 3.5 × 2.36 = 8.260
         (1 d.p.) + (2 d.p.) = (3 d.p.)

To round a decimal

When working with decimals*, it is often necessary to approximate the figure by rounding* up or down. Do this in exactly the same way as you round integers*, but round the number to the nearest tenth, hundredth, thousandth and so on, depending on how many decimal places* (d.p.) or significant figures* (s.f.) you want to use. For example, 63.537 8 can be rounded in various ways:

      63.538 (3 d.p.)
      63.54 (2 d.p.)
      64 (2 s.f.)

Rounding error

The inaccuracy introduced into a calculation that uses figures which have been rounded*. For example, if 0.694 73 is rounded to 0.69, the rounding error is 0.694 73 − 0.69, which is 0.004 73. In general, leave any rounding up or down until you have a finished answer. If you round answers at each stage of the calculation the final answer will be less accurate.

* **Cubing** 8 (**Cube number**); **Decimal, Decimal place, Decimal point** 19; **Fraction** 17; **Integers** 6; **Reciprocal** 18; **Rounding** 16; **Significant figure** 9; **Squaring** 8 (**Square number**); **Scientific notation** 23.

EXPONENTS & SCIENTIFIC NOTATION

It can be difficult to work out arithmetic and do rough calculations when working with very large or very small numbers. **Exponents** and scientific notation* allow us to write out these numbers in a more compact, manageable way.

Exponent

The small number written at the top right of another number to indicate multiplication by itself. The exponent tells you how many times the number should appear in the multiplication.

e.g.　$a^2 = a \times a$
　　　$a^3 = a \times a \times a$

(where a represents any number)

So,　$4^2 = 4 \times 4$
　　　$6^4 = 6 \times 6 \times 6 \times 6$

A negative exponent indicates the reciprocal* of the number with a positive version of the exponent.

e.g.　$a^{-n} = \dfrac{1}{a^n}$

(where a and n represent any number)

So,　$6^{-2} = \dfrac{1}{6^2}$

Fractional exponent

An exponent that is a fraction* rather than an integer*, e.g. $5^{\frac{1}{3}}$, which means $\sqrt[3]{5}$ (see *Laws of exponents 9*, on page 22).

Power

The value of a number raised to an **exponent**.

e.g.　$4^2 = 4 \times 4 = 16$

So, 16 is said to be the second power of 4.

The term "power" is also often used instead of **exponent**. For example, in 4^2, the number 4 is said to have been raised to the power of 2.

When a number is raised to the power of two, it is said to have been squared*. When a number is raised to the power of 3, it is said to have been cubed*.

Use the exponent keys on your scientific calculator to square a number (x^2) or to raise a number to any power (x^y).

*This expression takes a lot of space to write out in full. By using **exponents**, you can write the same expression as 6^{12}, which is much shorter, and easier to understand at a glance.*

Laws of Exponents

The rules that apply when working with exponents* are called the **laws of exponents**.

1. To multiply powers* of the same number, add the exponents.
$$a^n \times a^m = a^{n+m}$$
where a, n and m represent any number.

e.g. $4^2 \times 4^4 = 4^{2+4} = 4^6$

because $4^2 \times 4^4 = (4 \times 4) \times (4 \times 4 \times 4 \times 4)$
$$= 4^6$$

This method cannot be used to multiply powers of different numbers.

2. To divide powers* of the same number, subtract the exponents.
$$a^n \div a^m = a^{n-m}$$
where a, n and m represent any number.

e.g. $3^6 \div 3^2 = 3^{6-2} = 3^4$

because $3^6 \div 3^2$
$$= (3 \times 3 \times 3 \times 3 \times 3 \times 3) \div (3 \times 3)$$
$$= 3^4$$

Powers of different numbers cannot be divided in this way.

3. Any number to the power* of 1 is equal to itself.
$$a^1 = a$$
where a represents any number.

e.g. $3^1 = 3$

4. The number 1 raised to any power* is always 1.
$$1^n = 1$$
where n represents any number.

e.g. $1^6 = 1 \times 1 \times 1 \times 1 \times 1 \times 1 = 1$

5. Any number to the power* of 0 is equal to 1. This is sometimes called the **zero exponent rule**.
$$a^0 = 1$$
where a represents any number.

e.g. $2^0 = 1$

because (using the second law, above)
$$\frac{a^m}{a^m} = 1 \text{ and } \frac{a^m}{a^m} = a^{m-m} = a^0$$
so it follows that $a^0 = 1$

6. To raise a power* to a power, multiply the exponents.
$$(a^n)^m = a^{n \times m}$$
where a, n and m represent any number.

e.g. $(5^2)^3 = 5^{2 \times 3} = 5^6$

because $(5^2)^3 = 5^2 \times 5^2 \times 5^2$
$$= 5^{2+2+2} = 5^6$$

7. To raise a multiplication expression to a power*, raise each number in the expression to the power.
$$(a \times b)^n = a^n \times b^n$$
where a, b and n represent any number.

e.g. $(5 \times 3)^2 = 5^2 \times 3^2$

because $(5 \times 3)^2 = 15^2 = 225$

and $5^2 \times 3^2 = 25 \times 9 = 225$

8. To raise a division expression to a power*, raise each number in the expression to the power.
$$\left(\frac{a}{b}\right)^m = \frac{a^m}{b^m}$$
where a, b and m represent any number.

$$\left(\frac{3}{4}\right)^3 = \frac{3^3}{4^3}$$

because $\dfrac{3}{4} \times \dfrac{3}{4} \times \dfrac{3}{4} = \dfrac{27}{64}$

and $\dfrac{3^3}{4^3} = \dfrac{27}{64}$

9. Fractional exponents* can be multiplied and divided in the same way as other exponents.

e.g. $6^{\frac{1}{2}} \times 6^{\frac{1}{2}} = 6^{\frac{1}{2}+\frac{1}{2}} = 6^1 = 6$

It also follows that, if $6^{\frac{1}{2}} \times 6^{\frac{1}{2}} = 6$, then $6^{\frac{1}{2}}$ is the square root* of 6. This rule can be written as:
$$a^{\frac{1}{2}} = \sqrt{a}$$
This also applies to any number to the power* of $\frac{1}{3}$.

e.g. $5^{\frac{1}{3}} \times 5^{\frac{1}{3}} \times 5^{\frac{1}{3}} = 5^{\frac{1}{3}+\frac{1}{3}+\frac{1}{3}} = 5^1 = 5$

So, $5^{\frac{1}{3}}$ is the cube root* of 5. This rule can be written as:
$$a^{\frac{1}{3}} = \sqrt[3]{a}$$
The general rule is that fractional exponents give root terms.
$$a^{\frac{1}{n}} = \sqrt[n]{a} \quad \text{and} \quad a^{\frac{m}{n}} = \sqrt[n]{a^m}$$

* **Cube root** 11; **Decimal point** 19; **Exponent** 21; **Fractional index, Index** 21; **Mass** 72; **Power** 21; **Significant figure** 9; **Square root** 7.

Scientific notation

Scientific notation is a method of writing numbers in the form $a \times 10^n$, where a is greater than or equal to 1 and less than 10.

e.g. $63,000 = 6.3 \times 10^4$

Scientific notation is also known as **exponential notation**.

To write a number in scientific notation, place a decimal point* between the first and second significant figures*. This will give a number between 1 and 10. Next, find the required power* of ten by counting how many digits farther to the left or right the decimal point is in the new number compared with the old number.

If the new number is smaller than the original, the power of ten is positive. This is because the number would need increasing to return to its original form. If the new number is greater than the original, the power of ten is negative.

e.g. 683,000,000 written in scientific notation is:

The mass* of the Moon is a 23-digit number of kilograms. It can easily be written in scientific notation as 7.37×10^{22} kg.

Position of decimal point in new number

Position of decimal point in original number

$$6.83\,0\,0\,0\,0\,0\,0 \times 10^8$$

The decimal point is 8 digits farther to the left.

0.000 058 42 written in scientific notation is:

Position of decimal point in original number

Position of decimal point in new number

$$0\,0\,0\,0\,0\,5.842 \times 10^{-5}$$

The decimal point is 5 digits farther to the right.

Scientific notation is useful for comparing very large and very small numbers. For example, 97,430,000,000 written in scientific notation is 9.743×10^{10} and 785,300,000 is 7.853×10^8. By comparing the exponents*, you can see that 10^8 is smaller than 10^{10}, and so know the relative size of the numbers.

Calculators and scientific notation
Calculators often use scientific notation to display numbers that are longer than can be displayed in the window.

Scientific calculators have different ways of displaying scientific notation. For example, some use "E," "EE," "EX" or "EXP" to indicate "$\times$ 10 to the power* of..."Others give the answer in scientific notation.
e.g.

1.4567 $^{\text{EXP12}}$	means 1.4567×10^{12}
5.856 $^{\text{EX}-6}$	means 5.856×10^{-6}
32.25 ^{9}	means 32.25×10^9

EXP   *Use the exponent* key on your scientific calculator to multiply a number by a power* of 10.*

 Internet links For links to useful websites on **indices and powers**, go to *www.usborne-quicklinks.com*

RATIO AND PROPORTION

A **ratio** is a comparison of two quantities in a particular order. For example, if there are three girls and eight boys in a room, the ratio of girls to boys is said to be three to eight and the ratio of boys to girls is eight to three. Ratios are written with a colon (:), so the ratio eight to three is written 8 : 3. This could also be written as the fraction $\frac{8}{3}$.

The ratio of stars to circles is 5 : 4.

Unitary ratio
A ratio in which one of the terms is 1.
e.g.　1 : 3 and 8 : 1

Ratios with more than two terms
A ratio compares two quantities, so a ratio that contains, for example, three terms, *a* : *b* : *c* is a shortened way of expressing three separate comparisons, *a* : *b*, *b* : *c* and *a* : *c*.

Equivalent ratios or equal ratios
Two or more ratios that have the same value. For example, 4 : 6 and 8 : 12 are equivalent ratios because they can both be **simplified** to 2 : 3. To find equivalent ratios, multiply or divide each part of the ratio by the same number (called a **constant**).
e.g.　Some equivalent ratios of 2 : 4 are
　　　1 : 2　　　(divided by 2)
　　　4 : 8　　　(multiplied by 2)

To compare ratios
Express the ratios as fractions* with the same denominator* and then compare them.

For example, to find which is the larger ratio, 3 : 4 or 5 : 6, first express them as fractions, then rewrite the fractions in terms of their lowest common denominator*.

$$3 : 4 = \overset{\times 3}{\frac{3}{4}} = \frac{9}{12} \quad \text{and} \quad 5 : 6 = \overset{\times 2}{\frac{5}{6}} = \frac{10}{12}$$

$\frac{10}{12}$ is larger than $\frac{9}{12}$, so 5 : 6 is larger than 3 : 4.

If both parts of the ratio represent the same measurement, for example length, make sure that they are in the same units. It is usually best to convert the larger unit into the smaller one.
e.g. 1m : 47cm = 100cm : 47cm = 100 : 47

Simplifying ratios

Ratios can often be **simplified**, that is, expressed in smaller numbers or, in the case of fractions*, as integers*. To simplify a ratio, divide or multiply both parts by the same number so that the value of the ratio stays the same. When both parts of a ratio are as small as they can be, while still being integers, the ratio is said to be in its **simplest form**.

To simplify a whole number ratio
If necessary, make sure that both parts of the ratio are in the same units. The ratio can then be simplified by dividing both parts by their greatest common factor*.

For example, express in its simplest form the ratio 40min : 2h.

$$\begin{aligned} 40\text{min} : 2\text{h} &= 40\text{min} : 120\text{min} \ (2\text{h} = 120\text{min}) \\ &= 40 : 120 \\ &= 1 : 3 \ (\text{dividing each term by } 40) \end{aligned}$$

So, 40min : 2h in its simplest form is 1 : 3.

If the numbers in the ratio have no common factors*, e.g. 7 : 9, the ratio is already in its simplest form.

To simplify a ratio that includes a fraction
If necessary, make sure that both parts of the ratio are in the same units. Then multiply the fraction* to give an integer, and multiply the other part of the ratio by the same number. For example, to express $\frac{1}{2}$: 2 in its simplest form, multiply both sides by 2

$$\frac{1}{2} \times 2 = 1 \quad \text{and} \quad 2 \times 2 = 4$$

So, $\frac{1}{2}$: 2 in its simplest form is 1 : 4.

* **Common factor** 11; **Denominator, Fraction** 16; **Graph (Line graph)** 110; **Greatest common factor** 11 (**Common factor**); **Integers** 6; **Lowest common denominator** 17 (**Equivalent fractions**); **Product** 14 (**Multiplication**); **Reciprocal graph** 84; **Slope** 80.

Proportion

If two quantities change by a related amount, they are said to be **in proportion** or **proportional to** each other. The symbol that indicates proportion is $\propto$.

Direct proportion

A relationship between quantities, such that when one quantity increases, the other increases in the same ratio. Similarly when one quantity decreases, the other decreases in the same ratio.

For example, if one watermelon feeds eight people, the ratio of melons to people is 1 : 8.

Two melons would feed 16 people (2 $\times$ 8).

Half a melon would feed four people ($\frac{1}{2} \times$ 8).

The number of people fed is said to be in direct proportion, or **directly proportional**, to the number of watermelons.

When quantity a is directly proportional to quantity b, this is written as $a \propto b$. The fixed relationship between the quantities is called the **constant of proportionality** and the relationship can also be written as:
$$a = kb$$
where k is the constant of proportionality.

In the example above, the ratio of people (quantity a) to watermelons (quantity b) is 8 : 1, so the constant of proportionality is 8. This means that the number of people who can be fed is always eight times the number of melons.

Graph showing the number of watermelons needed to feed various numbers of people

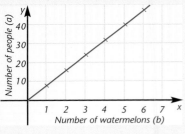

If you plot the values of a and b on a graph*, it gives a straight line which passes through (0,0) and has a slope* of k.

Inverse proportion

The relationship between quantities, such that when one quantity increases, the other decreases in the same ratio. Similarly, when one quantity decreases, the other increases in the same ratio.

For example, the table below shows how long it would take a car to travel a distance of 120km at various speeds.

Speed (kph)	20	40	60	80
Time (hours)	6	3	2	1.5

The time of the journey goes down as the speed goes up. This is an example of inverse proportion, and the time of the journey is said to be **inversely proportional** to the speed.

When quantity a is indirectly proportional to quantity b, this is written as $a \propto \frac{1}{b}$. The relationship can be also be written as:
$$a = \frac{k}{b} \quad \text{or} \quad a \times b = k$$
where k is the constant of proportionality.

In the example above, the product* of the time (quantity a) and the speed (quantity b) is always the same (e.g. 20 $\times$ 6 = 120 and 40 $\times$ 30 = 120), so the **constant of proportionality** is 120. This means that for the 120km journey, the time taken will always be equal to 120 divided by the speed.

All examples of inverse proportion can be expressed by the rule:

The product of two inversely proportional quantities is constant.

Graph showing the time taken to travel 120km at various speeds

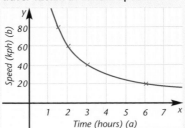

If you plot the values of a and b on a graph*, the result is a reciprocal graph*, which is a curve.

Solving ratio problems

To divide a quantity in a given ratio
1. Add all the numbers in the ratio* to find out what the total number of parts is.
2. Divide the quantity by the total number of parts to find the value of one part.
3. Multiply each number in the ratio in turn by the value of one part to find out the value of each share.

For example, if angles *a*, *b* and *c* in this triangle are in the ratio 4 : 3 : 5, what is the size of each angle?

Total number of parts = 4 + 3 + 5 = 12
Total number of degrees in the triangle = 180

One part is $\frac{180}{12} = 15°$

Angle *a* is $4 \times 15 = 60°$
Angle *b* is $3 \times 15 = 45°$
Angle *c* is $5 \times 15 = 75°$

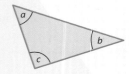

To divide a line in a given ratio
A line can be divided internally or externally in a given ratio*. If the point P lies between A and B on the line that joins them, the line AB is said to be divided **internally**. The first number in the ratio represents AP and the second number represents PB.

e.g.

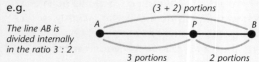

The line AB is divided internally in the ratio 3 : 2.

(3 + 2) portions

3 portions   2 portions

If point P lies on the continuation of the line AB (known as AB or BA **produced**), the line is said to be divided **externally**. If the first part of the ratio is larger than the second, P is closer to B than A and is on the line AB produced.

e.g. (3 − 2) portions   2 portions

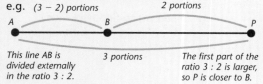

This line AB is divided externally in the ratio 3 : 2.

3 portions

The first part of the ratio 3 : 2 is larger, so P is closer to B.

If the second part of the ratio is larger, P is closer to A than B and is on the line BA produced.

e.g.   2 portions   (3 − 2) portions

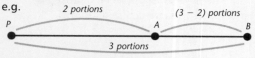

3 portions

This line AB is divided externally in the ratio 2 : 3.

Solving proportion problems

Unitary method
A method of solving problems where one quantity is proportional* to another, by finding the value of one unit of a quantity and multiplying it to find the value of a required number of units.

For example, a printing press prints 200 pages every 5 minutes. How many pages will it print in 3 hours?

1. Find out how many pages it prints in one minute:
   In 5 minutes, the press prints 200 pages.
   In 1 minute, it will print $\frac{200}{5}$ pages.
   The press will print 40 pages in 1 minute.
2. Find out how many minutes there are in 3 hours:
   1 hour = 60 minutes
   $\therefore$ 3 hours = 180 minutes

In 180 minutes (3 hours) the press will print 180×40 pages, that is, 7,200 pages.

Ratio method
A method of solving problems using direct proportion*. In this method, the ratios* are shown as fractions*, where the numerator* of one of the fractions (*x*) is unknown. The value of *x* can then be found by multiplying both fractions by the same number.

For example, a printing press prints 200 pages every 5 minutes. How many pages will it print in 3 hours?

The number of pages printed in 3 hours is directly proportional* to the number of pages printed in 5 minutes. Let *x* be the number of pages printed in 180 minutes (3 hours).

$$\frac{x}{180} = \frac{200}{5}$$

$$\overset{1}{\cancel{180}} \times \frac{x}{\cancel{180}_1} = 180 \times \frac{200}{5}$$

$$x = 180 \times \frac{200}{5}$$

$$x = \frac{36,000}{5}$$

$$x = 7,200$$

So, the press can print 7,200 pages in 3 hours.

* **Cancel** 17 (Equivalent fractions); **Decimal, Decimal point** 19; **Direct proportion** 25; **Fraction** 17; **Lowest possible terms** (Equivalent fractions) 17; **Numerator** 17; **Proportional** 25; **Ratio** 24.

PERCENTAGES

A **percentage** is a way of expressing a fraction* or decimal* as parts of a hundred: **per cent** means "in each hundred." For example, 10 percent (10%) means $\frac{10}{100}$ or 10 hundredths.

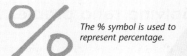

The % symbol is used to represent percentage.

%

Use the percentage key on your calculator to find a percentage of a number.

To change a fraction or decimal to a percentage

Multiply the fraction or decimal by 100.

e.g. $\frac{3}{4} = \left(\frac{3}{4} \times 100\right)\% = \frac{300}{4}\% = 75\%$

$0.28 = (0.28 \times 100)\% = 28\%$

In both examples above, the fraction and decimal are less than 1, so the equivalent percentage is less than 100%. A fraction or decimal that is greater than 1 always converts to a percentage that is greater than 100%.

e.g. $2\frac{1}{5} = \left(\frac{11}{5} \times 100\right)\%$

$= \frac{1100}{5}$

$= \frac{220}{1}$

$= 220\%$

and $\quad 1.16 = (1.16 \times 100)\% = 116\%$

To change a percentage to a fraction

Divide the percentage by 100, then cancel* the fraction down to its lowest possible terms*.

e.g. $60\% = \frac{60}{100} = \frac{3}{5}$

To change a percentage to a decimal

Divide the percentage by 100.

e.g. $60\% = 0.6$

$5.2\% = 0.052$

To find a percentage of a known quantity

Express the percentage as a fraction $(\frac{x}{100})$ and multiply it by the quantity. Alternatively, express the percentage as a decimal and multiply it by the quantity.

For example, 5% of the population of a town where 9,000 people live is:

$\frac{5}{100} \times 9,000 = 450$

or $\quad 0.05 \times 9,000 = 450$

To express one quantity as a percentage of another

Divide one quantity by the other and multiply the result by 100.

$$\text{Percentage} = \frac{\text{Quantity A}}{\text{Quantity B}} \times 100\%$$

For example, in one day, 51 of the 60 buses that stopped at a bus station were on time. What percentage of buses were on time?

$$\frac{\text{Buses on time}}{\text{Total number of buses}} \times 100\%$$

$\frac{51}{60} \times 100\% = 85\%$

85% of buses were on time.

To find an original quantity

Divide the known quantity by the percentage (to find 1% of the original quantity), then multiply it by 100 (to find the whole quantity). Alternatively, divide the known quantity by the percentage written as a decimal. These methods are sometimes called **reverse percentages**.

For example, 75% of pupils in a class passed a test. If 24 pupils passed, how many pupils are in the class?

Either:
Divide 24 by 75 percent to find how many pupils make up 1% of the class then multiply by 100 to find the total number in the class:

$\frac{24}{75} \times 100 = 32$

or:
Divide the number of pupils who passed by the percentage expressed as a decimal:

$24 \div 0.75 = 32$

There are 32 children in the class.

Internet links For links to useful websites on **percentages**, go to *www.usborne-quicklinks.com*

Percentage change

The amount that a value has changed, expressed as a percentage* of the original value, is called **percentage change**.

$$\text{Percentage change} = \frac{\text{new value} - \text{original value}}{\text{original value}} \times 100$$

Percentage increase

A positive percentage change. A percentage increase can be calculated using:

$$\text{Percentage increase} = \frac{\text{increase in value}}{\text{original value}} \times 100$$

For example, a school with 750 pupils receives funding for another 75 places. Express this rise as a percentage increase.

$$\begin{aligned}
\text{Percentage increase} &= \frac{75}{750} \times 100 \\
&= \frac{1}{10} \times 100 \\
&= \frac{100}{10} \\
&= 10
\end{aligned}$$

The rise in number of places that can be offered at the school is a percentage increase of 10%.

Percentage decrease

A negative percentage change. A percentage decrease can be calculated using:

$$\text{Percentage decrease} = \frac{\text{decrease in value}}{\text{original value}} \times 100$$

For example, one year a factory produces 60 cars per worker. The following year this total has fallen to 57 cars per worker. What is the percentage decrease?

Decrease in cars per worker = 60 − 57 = 3

$$\begin{aligned}
\text{Percentage decrease} &= \frac{3}{60} \times 100 \\
&= \frac{1}{20} \times 100 \\
&= \frac{100}{20} \\
&= 5
\end{aligned}$$

The fall in the factory's output represents a percentage decrease of 5%.

Interest

When you put money into a savings account in a bank or credit union, the bank or credit union uses that money, for example by lending it to other people. The bank or credit union pays you a certain amount, called **interest**, for letting them use your money.

Similarly, when you borrow money from a bank or credit union, you will have to pay them a certain amount of interest, as well as paying back the amount you borrowed. The amount originally borrowed or lent is called the **principal**.

The **rate of interest** (or **interest rate**) is the amount of interest charged or earned in a year. It is expressed as a **percentage* per annum** (p.a.) of the principal. (*Per annum* means "in each year".) For example, an interest rate of 4% p.a. means that every $100 invested gains $4 (which is 4% of $100) at the end of the year.

There are two types of interest: simple and compound interest. These are calculated in different ways.

Simple interest

Interest that is earned or paid only on the **principal** without including any earlier interest earned. The amount that earns interest does not change.

Compound interest

Interest that is earned or paid on an original sum of money invested, including the interest already earned. The amount of money that earns interest increases each year.

Multiplier

A number that, when multiplied by a **principal**, gives the total amount saved or borrowed at the end of a period of time (usually a year), including interest. The multiplier is 1 plus the rate of interest expressed as a decimal*. For example, the multiplier for an interest rate of 6% p.a. is 1.06.

*Decimal 19; Percentage 27.

To calculate simple interest

$$\text{Simple interest} = \frac{P \times R \times T}{100}$$

where P is the **principal**, R is the **rate of interest** (as a percentage*) and T is the time (in years) over which interest is being calculated.

To find the total amount in the account, use:

$$\text{Total amount} = P + \frac{P \times R \times T}{100}$$

For example, if a person invests $500 at an interest rate of 4% per annum, the amount of interest earned each year is $20, because:

$$\frac{500 \times 4 \times 1}{100} = 20$$

The total amount in the account at the end of the first year is $520 (the interest added to the principal).

To calculate compound interest
(Long method)

Use a **multiplier** to find the total amount including interest at the end of each year, then use this new amount as the principal for the following year.

For example, if a person invests $500 at a compound interest rate of 4% p.a., the amount in the account at the end of the year is $520 ($500 × 1.04). In the second year, interest is calculated on a new amount, $520 (the original $500 investment plus the 4% interest), and so on.

Year 1 amount = $500 × 1.04 = $520
Year 2 amount = $520 × 1.04 = $540.80
Year 3 amount = $540.80 × 1.04 = $562.43 (2 d.p.)

This method of calculating compound interest over a large number of years is time-consuming. An alternative method is explained opposite.

To calculate compound interest
(Short method)

Consider that a person invests $500 in a savings account that pays interest at a rate of 5% p.a.

At the end of year 1, the new amount is:
$500 × 1.05
(principal × multiplier)

At the end of year 2, the amount is:
($500 × 1.05) × 1.05
$= \$500 \times 1.05^2$

At the end of year 3, the amount is:
($500 × 1.05) × 1.05 × 1.05
$= \$500 \times 1.05^3$

This sequence can be used to calculate the amount in the account:

after 6 years	$500 × 1.05^6
after 10 years	$500 × 1.05^{10}
after n years	$500 × 1.05^n

The power to which the multiplier is raised is called the **multiplying factor**, and it is the same as the number of years an investment is earning interest. So, to find the total amount in an account earning compound interest, use:

$$\text{Total amount} = P \times \left(1 + \frac{R}{100}\right)^T$$

$$\text{Compound interest} = P \times \left(1 + \frac{R}{100}\right)^T - P$$

where P is the **principal**, R is the **percentage rate of interest** and T is the time (in years) over which interest is being calculated.

For example, $20 invested for five years at 4% interest would be $24.33 (2 d.p.):

$$20 \times (1.04)^5$$
$$= 20 \times 1.2167$$
$$= 24.334$$
$$= 24.33 \ (2 \ d.p.)$$

GEOMETRY

Geometry is the study of the properties of shapes and the space around them, from a simple triangle to the most complex solid.

Triangle

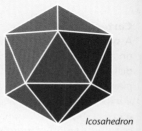

Geometry is the study of shapes, such as this triangle and icosahedron, and the relationships between them.

Icosahedron

Point

A location that can be described by giving its **coordinates**. A point has no length, width or thickness. It is usually represented on diagrams by a small dot or two crossed lines.

Line segment

The part of a straight line between two **points**. A line segment has a fixed length. Strictly speaking, a **line** continues indefinitely in both directions. Lines and line segments are **one dimensional**: they have length but no width or thickness.

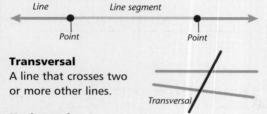

Line   Line segment

Point   Point

Transversal

A line that crosses two or more other lines.

Transversal

Horizontal

A way of describing a **line** or **plane** that follows the horizon, at a right angle (90°) to the **vertical**.

Vertical

A way of describing a **line** or **plane** that is at a right angle (90°) to the horizon.

Perpendicular

A way of describing a **line** or **plane** that is at a right angle (90°) to another line or plane.

Parallel

A way of describing a set of **lines** or curves that never meet, however far they are extended. They are the same distance apart all the way along.

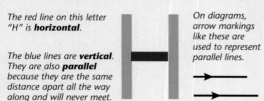

The red line on this letter "H" is **horizontal**.

The blue lines are **vertical**. They are also **parallel** because they are the same distance apart all the way along and will never meet.

On diagrams, arrow markings like these are used to represent parallel lines.

Collinear

A way of describing **points** that lie in a straight line, or share a common straight line.

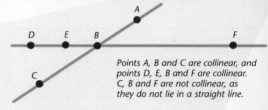

Points A, B and C are collinear, and points D, E, B and F are collinear. C, B and F are not collinear, as they do not lie in a straight line.

Plane or plane figure

A **two-dimensional** object, with length and width

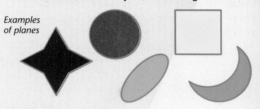

Examples of planes

Coplanar

A way of describing **points** that lie on the same **plane**, or share a common plane.

In this shape, points A, C and D are coplanar, and points A, B and E are coplanar. However, A, B, C and D are not coplanar because they do not share a common plane.

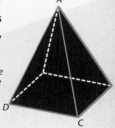

Solid

A **three-dimensional** object, with length, width and thickness.

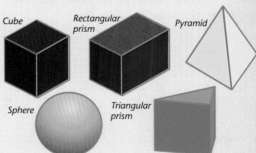

Cube   Rectangular prism   Pyramid

Sphere   Triangular prism

Cartesian coordinate system

A system of describing the position of **points** on a **plane** or in a space in terms of their distance from lines called **axes**. Points on a plane are described in terms of two lines, the **x-axis** and the **y-axis**, which are at right angles (90°) to each other to form a **rectangular coordinate system**.

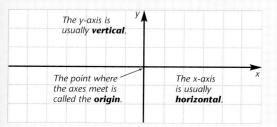

The y-axis is usually **vertical**.

The point where the axes meet is called the **origin**.

The x-axis is usually **horizontal**.

Distances along the *x*-axis to the right of the origin are usually positive, and those along the *x*-axis to the left of the origin are negative. Distances along the *y*-axis above the origin are positive and those below the origin are negative.

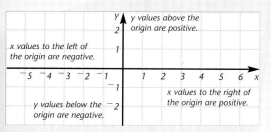

y values above the origin are positive.

x values to the left of the origin are negative.

y values below the origin are negative.

x values to the right of the origin are positive.

Cartesian coordinates

The **coordinates** (x, y), which describe the position of a point in terms of its distance from the origin. The **x-coordinate** is the distance of the point from the origin, **parallel** to the *x*-axis. The **y-coordinate** is the distance of the point from the origin, parallel to the *y*-axis. The *x*-coordinate is always written first.

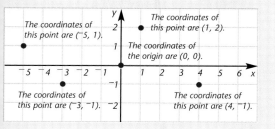

The coordinates of this point are (⁻5, 1).

The coordinates of this point are (1, 2).

The coordinates of the origin are (0, 0).

The coordinates of this point are (⁻3, ⁻1).

The coordinates of this point are (4, ⁻1).

Quadrant

Any of the four regions formed on a **plane** by the **x-axis** and **y-axis**. (Quadrant is also the name of part of a circle, see page 65.)

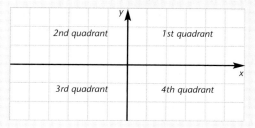

2nd quadrant | 1st quadrant

3rd quadrant | 4th quadrant

Dimensions

The number of **coordinates** needed to fix a **point** in a space.

The position of a point on a **line** or **line segment** can be described by one coordinate. This means that a line is **one-dimensional**.

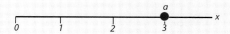

The position of point a is 3.

Two coordinates are needed to describe the position of a point in a **plane**, so a plane is **two-dimensional**.

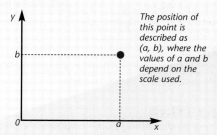

The position of this point is described as (a, b), where the values of a and b depend on the scale used.

Three coordinates are needed to describe the position of a point in a space. This means that the space around us, or a solid shape within that space is **three-dimensional**.

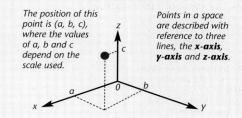

The position of this point is (a, b, c), where the values of a, b and c depend on the scale used.

Points in a space are described with reference to three lines, the **x-axis**, **y-axis** and **z-axis**.

ANGLES

An **angle** is formed wherever two lines meet at a point*. The angle is measured by the amount of turn that one line must travel about this point to arrive at the position of the other line. This turn is measured in **degrees** (°). There are several types of angles, classified by their size.

An angle is formed between two lines, called the **arms** of the angle.

Null angle or **zero angle**

No rotation (0°).

Obtuse angle

Any angle greater than a right angle (90°), but smaller than a straight angle (180°).

90° < angle < 180°

Whole turn, full turn, round angle or **perigon**

A complete turn, or **revolution**, equal to 360°.

Reflex angle

Any angle greater than a straight angle (180°).

Right angle

A quarter of a **full turn**, equal to 90°. Lines that meet at a right angle are described as **perpendicular**.

These lines are perpendicular.

This symbol is used to show that an angle is a right angle.

The minute hand of a clock turns a complete revolution, 360°, every hour. The direction in which the hands travel around the clock is described as **clockwise**. The opposite direction is **counter-clockwise**.

Clockwise   Counter-clockwise

Straight angle or **flat angle**

Half a **full turn**, equal to 180°.

Positive angle
An angle that is constructed or measured in a counter-clockwise direction.

This angle is measured counter-clockwise, so it is positive (+100°).

Acute angle

Any angle smaller than a right angle (90°).

0° < angle < 90°

Negative angle
An angle that is constructed or measured in a clockwise direction.

This angle is measured clockwise, so it is negative (⁻100°).

* **Cyclic quadrilateral** 71; **Parallel, Point** 30; **Right-angled triangle** 37; **Transversal** 30; **Vertex** 34 (**Polygons**).

Pairs of angles

As well as being defined by their size, angles can be named and grouped by their relationship to lines and other angles. Many of the types of angles described below come in pairs.

Adjacent angles

Angles that share a vertex* (point) and a line.

Angles a and b are adjacent: they share vertex V and line VL.

Alternate angles

Angles formed on alternate sides of a transversal* between parallel* lines. Alternate angles are equal.

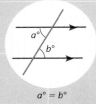

$a° = b°$

$c° = d°$

Angles at a point*

The angles formed when any number of lines meet at a point. These angles add up to 360°.

$a° + b° + c° = 360°$

$a° + b° + c° + d° + e° = 360°$

Complementary angles

Two angles that add up to 90°. Each angle is said to be the **complement** of the other.

$a° + b° = 90°$

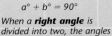

When a **right angle** is divided into two, the angles formed are complementary.

$a° + b° = 90°$

In a right-angled triangle*, the angles a and b are complementary.

Corresponding angles

Angles that have a similar position with relation to a transversal* and one of a pair of parallel* lines. A transversal across parallel lines produces four pairs of corresponding angles. Corresponding angles are equal.

$a° = b°$

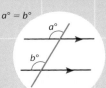

$c° = d°$

The four pairs of corresponding angles created by a transversal* and parallel* lines

$e° = f°$

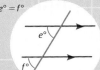

$g° = h°$

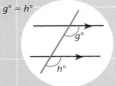

Supplementary angles

Two angles that add up to 180°. Each angle is said to be the **supplement** of the other.

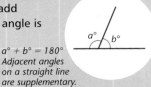

$a° + b° = 180°$
Adjacent angles on a straight line are supplementary.

$a° + b° = 180°$

The angles between parallel* lines and a transversal* are supplementary.

$a° + b° = 180°$

The opposite angles of a cyclic quadrilateral* are supplementary.

Vertically opposite angles

The angles on opposite sides of the point where two lines cross. These pairs of angles are always equal.

$a° = c°$ and $b° = d°$

POLYGONS

A **polygon** is a shape formed from three or more points* joined by three or more straight lines. The points are known as **vertices** (each point is a **vertex**), and the lines are called **sides**. The name of most polygons relates to the number of angles* or sides it has.

Name of polygon	Number of angles and sides	Shape
Triangle	3	
Quadrilateral	4	
Pentagon	5	
Hexagon	6	
Heptagon or septagon	7	
Octagon	8	
Nonagon	9	
Decagon	10	
Hendecagon	11	
Dodecagon	12	
Quindecagon	15	
Icosagon	20	

N-gon

A polygon that has n angles and n sides, where n represents any number.

Interior angle

Any of the angles inside a polygon, where two sides meet at a vertex. The sum of the interior angles of a polygon is equal to the sum of the interior angles of any other polygon with the same number of sides. The sum of the interior angles in an n-sided polygon is $180° (n - 2)$.

e.g.

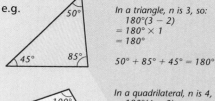

In a triangle, n is 3, so:
$$180°(3 - 2)$$
$$= 180° \times 1$$
$$= 180°$$

$50° + 85° + 45° = 180°$

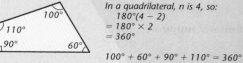

In a quadrilateral, n is 4, so:
$$180°(4 - 2)$$
$$= 180° \times 2$$
$$= 360°$$

$100° + 60° + 90° + 110° = 360°$

Exterior angle or external angle

Any of the angles formed between a side of a polygon and the extension of the side next to it.

An interior angle and the exterior angle next to it are supplementary – they always add up to 180°.*

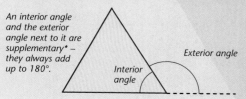

Interior angle

Exterior angle

Diagonal

A line that joins two vertices of a polygon that are not next to each other.

Diagonals

Cyclic

A polygon that can have a circle drawn around it such that each vertex of the polygon lies on the circle's circumference*.

A cyclic quadrilateral

* **Acute angle, Angle** 32; **Circumference** 65; **Obtuse angle** 32; **Point** 30; **Rectangle** 39; **Reflex** 32; **Rhombus** 39; **Supplementary** 33.

Equiangular polygon

A polygon in which all the **interior angles** are equal. An equiangular polygon does not have to be **equilateral**.

This rectangle* is equiangular, as all of its angles are right angles (90°). However, it is not equilateral as the lengths of its sides vary.

Equilateral polygon

A polygon in which all the sides are equal. An equilateral polygon does not have to be **equiangular**.

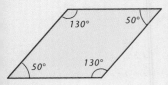

This rhombus* is equilateral, as all its sides are equal in length. However, its interior angles are different so it is not equiangular.

Convex polygon

A polygon in which all **interior angles** are less than 180°.

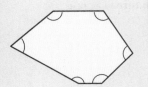

Every interior angle in a convex polygon is acute* or obtuse* (less than 180°).

Concave polygon

A polygon in which one or more **interior angle** is greater than 180°.

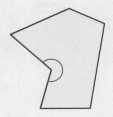

At least one interior angle in a concave polygon is reflex* (more than 180°).

Regular polygon

A polygon in which all the sides and **interior angles** are equal: it is both **equiangular** and **equilateral**. Here are some examples of regular polygons:

Equilateral triangle

Square

Regular pentagon

Regular hexagon

The Pentagon, in Washington, DC, USA, is the headquarters of the United States Department of Defense. The building is named after its five-sided shape.

Labeling polygons

The vertices of a polygon are often represented by upper-case letters (e.g. A, B, C ...) and the sides by lower-case letters (e.g. a, b, c ...).

The side of a polygon directly opposite a vertex is represented by the same letter but in lower case.

Internet links For links to useful websites on **shapes and solids**, go to *www.usborne-quicklinks.com*

Tessellation

Tessellation is the combination of one or more shapes such that, when repeated, the pattern covers a surface without leaving any gaps or overlaps. Shapes that fit together in this way are said to **tessellate**.

These squares tessellate.

These circles don't tessellate.

Many shapes tessellate, but there are two kinds of tessellation that involve only regular polygons*: regular and semi-regular tessellation.

Regular tessellation

A tessellation made up of only one type of regular polygon.

There are three regular polygons that will form a regular tessellation: an equilateral triangle, square and regular hexagon.

Semi-regular tessellation

A tessellation made up of more than one type of regular polygon. The pattern formed at each vertex (point) where the polygons meet is the same.

There are eight semi-regular tessellations. These use a combination of equilateral triangles, squares, hexagons, octagons and dodecagons.

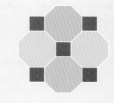

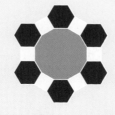

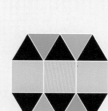

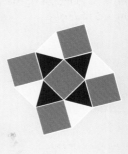

** **Exterior angle, Interior angle** 34; **Line of symmetry** 42;
Regular polygon 35; **Vertex** 34 (**Polygons**).*

Triangles

A **triangle** is a polygon with three angles and therefore three sides. If some of the angles and sides of a triangle are known, others can be calculated using the *Pythagorean theorem* (see page 38) and *trigonometry* (see pages 60–64).

Triangles can be classified according to the lengths of their sides.

Equal sides
An equal number of dash marks on two or more sides of a shape identify the sides that are of equal length.

Scalene triangle

A triangle in which the sides are all different lengths, and all three angles are different. A scalene triangle can also be a **right-angled triangle**.

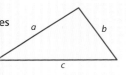

In a scalene triangle, sides a, b and c are different lengths.

Isosceles triangle

A triangle that has two equal sides. The angles opposite these sides are also equal. *Isosceles* is a Greek word, meaning "equal legs." An isosceles triangle has one line of symmetry*, which divides the triangle into two identical **right-angled triangles**.

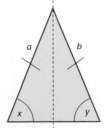

This is an isosceles triangle: angles x and y are equal, and sides a and b are equal.

Equilateral triangle

A triangle that has three equal sides. Each angle measures 60°.

An equilateral triangle has three lines of symmetry, each of which divides the triangle into two identical **right-angled triangles**.

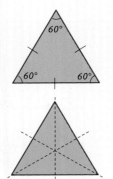

Triangles can also be classified according to their angles.

Acute-angled triangle

A triangle in which all three interior angles* are acute, that is, less than 90°.

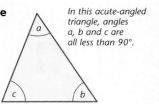

In this acute-angled triangle, angles a, b and c are all less than 90°.

Obtuse-angled triangle

A triangle in which one interior angle* is obtuse, that is, greater than 90°.

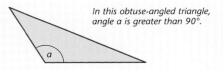

In this obtuse-angled triangle, angle a is greater than 90°.

Right-angled triangle

A triangle in which one interior angle* is a right angle, that is, 90°. The other two angles are complementary, which means that they add up to 90°.

A right-angled triangle has special properties (see Pythagorean theorem, on page 38).

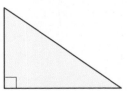

Angles in a triangle

The interior angles* add up to 180°:
$a° + b° + c° = 180°$

Each exterior angle* is equal to the sum of the two opposite interior angles:
$d° = a° + c°$

The top vertex* of a triangle is called the **apex**.

An angle formed between two sides is called the **included angle**.

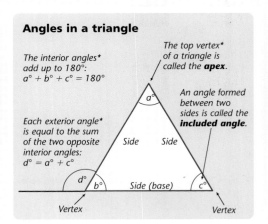

More triangles

Congruent triangles
Triangles that are exactly the same shape and size. Two triangles are congruent* if they meet any of the conditions described below.

Side-side-side (SSS)
If all three sides of one triangle are equal to all three sides of another triangle, the triangles are congruent.

Side-angle-side (SAS)
If two sides and the included angle* of one triangle are the same as two sides and the included angle of another triangle, the triangles are congruent.

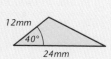

Angle-angle-side (AAS)
If two angles and any side of one triangle are the same as two angles and any side of another triangle, the triangles are congruent.

Right-angle-hypotenuse-side (RHS)
If the hypotenuse (longest side of a right-angled triangle*) and one side of a right-angled triangle are the same as the hypotenuse and one side of another right-angled triangle, the triangles are congruent.

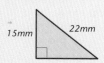

Similar* triangles
Triangles that are the same shape but not necessarily the same size. Corresponding angles are equal and corresponding sides are in the same ratio.

Pythagorean theorem
A theorem attributed to a Greek philosopher and mathematician named Pythagoras who lived in the sixth century BC. The theorem states that in a right-angled triangle*, the square* of the hypotenuse is equal to the sum* of the squares of the other two sides.
The **hypotenuse** is the longest side of a right-angled triangle. This is always the side opposite the right angle (the 90° angle).

The Pythagorean theorem can be written as:
$$a^2 + b^2 = c^2$$

If the square of one side of a triangle is equal to the sum of the squares of the other two sides, the theorem shows that the triangle must contain a right angle.

$$a^2 + b^2 = c^2$$
$$3^2 + 4^2 = 5^2$$
$$9 + 16 = 25$$

Therefore, we know that angle x opposite the hypotenuse must be a right angle.

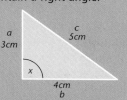

The theorem can be used to find the length of the third side of a right-angled triangle, if the lengths of any two sides are known.

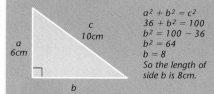

$$a^2 + b^2 = c^2$$
$$36 + b^2 = 100$$
$$b^2 = 100 - 36$$
$$b^2 = 64$$
$$b = 8$$
So the length of side b is 8cm.

Pythagorean triple or triad
A set of three positive integers* (a, b and c) representing the sides of a triangle and satisfying the **Pythagorean theorem** ($a^2 + b^2 = c^2$).

There is an infinite number of Pythagorean triples. The most well known are:
$$3, 4, 5: \quad 3^2 + 4^2 = 5^2$$
$$5, 12, 13: \quad 5^2 + 12^2 = 13^2$$
$$7, 24, 25: \quad 7^2 + 24^2 = 25^2$$
$$8, 15, 17: \quad 8^2 + 15^2 = 17^2$$

Quadrilaterals

A four-sided polygon is called a **quadrilateral** ("quad" means "four"). All quadrilaterals tessellate*. The quadrilaterals listed on this page have special properties.

Square

A quadrilateral in which all sides are equal and all angles are right angles (90°). The opposite sides of a square are parallel*. A square has four lines of symmetry* and rotation symmetry* of order 4.

A square has 4 sides of equal length and 4 right angles.

The opposite sides of a square are parallel, and its diagonals are of equal length.*

A square has 4 lines of symmetry and rotation symmetry of order 4.

Rectangle

A quadrilateral in which opposite sides are equal and parallel*, and all interior angles* are right angles (90°). A rectangle has 2 lines of symmetry* and rotation symmetry* of order 2. The diagonals* of a rectangle are equal in length. A rectangle is also sometimes known as an **oblong**.

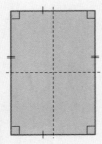

A rectangle has 2 lines of symmetry and rotation symmetry of order 2.

Kite

A quadrilateral that has two pairs of equal sides and one pair of opposite equal angles. It has only one line of symmetry* and no rotation symmetry*.

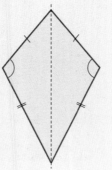

A kite has one pair of equal angles. It has one line of symmetry.

Parallelogram

A quadrilateral in which opposite sides are parallel* and equal in length, and opposite angles are equal. Most parallelograms have no lines of symmetry* and have rotation symmetry* of order 2. The exceptions are **rectangles**, **squares** and **rhombuses**, which are special types of parallelograms.

The opposite angles of this parallelogram are equal. It does not contain any right angles.

Rhombus

A **parallelogram** in which all four sides are equal in length, and opposite angles are equal. A rhombus has two lines of symmetry* and rotation symmetry* of order 2. A **square** is a special type of rhombus, as it has four right angles.

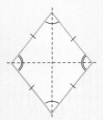

*A rhombus is sometimes called a **diamond** when it is standing on a vertex.*

Trapezoid

A quadrilateral that has one pair of parallel* sides. Most trapezoids have no symmetry*. However, if the sloping sides *a* and *b* of a trapezoid are the same length, it has one line of symmetry*. A trapezoid of this type is an **isosceles trapezoid**.

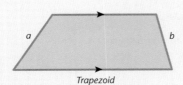

Trapezoid

Arrowhead

Arrowhead or delta

A concave* quadrilateral with two pairs of equal adjacent sides. An arrowhead has one interior angle* greater than 180°, and one line of symmetry*. It has no rotation symmetry*.

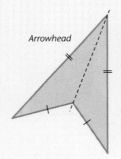

SOLIDS

A **solid** is a three-dimensional* object. A solid can be any shape or size, but many solids, such as **polyhedra**, spheres, cylinders and cones, have particular properties. The properties of polyhedra are described below, and you can find out more about cylinders, cones and spheres on pages 67–69.

Polyhedron (plural is polyhedra)

A solid that has a surface area which is a series of polygons. The polygons are known as **faces** and the lines where they meet are called **edges**. The corners, where three or more faces meet, are called **vertices** (singular is **vertex**).

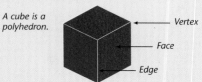

A cube is a polyhedron. — Vertex — Face — Edge

The name of a polyhedron is related to the number of faces it has.

Name of polyhedron	Number of faces
Tetrahedron	4
Pentahedron	5
Hexahedron	6
Heptahedron	7
Octahedron	8
Nonahedron	9
Decahedron	10
Dodecahedron	12
Icosahedron	20

Dihedral angle

The angle* formed inside a **polyhedron** where two **faces** meet.

Dihedral angle

Convex polyhedron

A **polyhedron** in which each **dihedral angle** is less than 180°, for example, a **cube**.

Concave polyhedron

A **polyhedron** in which at least one **dihedral angle** is greater than 180°. This means that at least one **vertex** points in toward the middle of the solid.

Concave polyhedron

Regular polyhedron

A **polyhedron** in which the **faces** are identical regular polygons*. The angles at the **vertices** are equal. There are five regular polyhedra. They were known to the Greek philosopher Plato, and are sometimes called the **Platonic solids**.

*A **regular tetrahedron** has four faces, which are equilateral triangles*.*

*A **cube** has six square faces.*

*A **regular octahedron** has eight faces, all of which are equilateral triangles*.*

*A **regular dodecahedron** has twelve faces, all of which are regular pentagons*.*

*A **regular icosahedron** has 20 faces, all of which are equilateral triangles*.*

Semi-regular polyhedron

A **polyhedron** in which the **faces** are more than one type of regular polygon. An **icosidodecahedron** is a semi-regular polyhedron with 32 faces: 20 triangles* and 12 pentagons*.

Icosidodecahedron

Euler's theorem

The theorem relating to **polyhedra**, such that:

$$V - E + F = 2$$

where V = number of **vertices**, E = number of **edges** and F = number of **faces**. This theorem can be demonstrated, for example, with a **cube**, which has 8 vertices, 12 edges and 6 faces ($8 - 12 + 6 = 2$). The theorem is named after the Swiss mathematician Leonard Euler (1707–83).

* **Angle** 32; **Axis of rotational symmetry** 42; **Equilateral triangle** 37; **Parallel** 30; **Pentagon** 35 (**Regular polygon**); **Perpendicular height** 56 (**Area of a triangle**); **Polygon** 34; **Regular polygon** 35; **Right angle** 32; **Three-dimensional** 31 (**Dimension**); **Triangle** 37; **Two-dimensional** 31 (**Dimension**).

Pyramid

A **polyhedron** with a polygonal base and triangular sides, which meet at an **apex** (the top vertex). The name of a pyramid relates to the shape of its base. If the base is a regular polygon*, the pyramid is a **regular pyramid**.

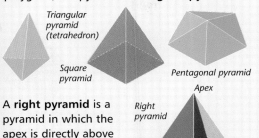

Triangular pyramid (tetrahedron)

Square pyramid

Pentagonal pyramid

A **right pyramid** is a pyramid in which the apex is directly above the middle of the base.

Apex

Right pyramid

Slant height

The length of a line drawn from the **apex** of a **pyramid** to the midpoint of the base **edge**. The slant height of a pyramid is equal to the perpendicular height* of the triangular face.

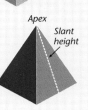

Apex

Slant height

Prism

A **polyhedron** made up of two parallel*, identical polygons* (the **bases**) joined by parallelograms (the **lateral faces**).

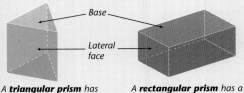

Base

Lateral face

*A **triangular prism** has a triangle as its base.*

*A **rectangular prism** has a rectangle as its base.*

In a **right prism**, the lateral faces are at right angles* to the base. If the bases of a right prism are regular polygons, the solid is a **regular prism**.

This right prism is a regular prism because its base is a square.

Right angle

Oblique prism

In an **oblique prism**, the angles between the lateral faces and the bases are not right angles.

Plan

A two-dimensional* drawing of a solid as if viewed directly from above.

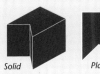

Solid

Plan

Elevation

A two-dimensional* drawing of a solid as if viewed directly from the front (**front elevation**), or the side (**side elevation**). The front is taken to be the face nearest to you.

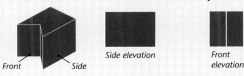

Front

Side

Side elevation

Front elevation

Diagonal

A line drawn between two **vertices** of a solid that are not on the same edge. Solids have **short diagonals**, which lie across the surface, and **long diagonals**, which run through the middle of the solid.

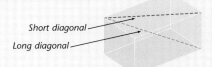

Short diagonal

Long diagonal

Plane section

A plane (flat) surface formed by cutting through a solid at any angle.

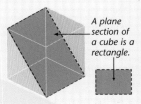

A plane section of a cube is a rectangle.

Cross section

A plane (flat) surface formed by cutting through a solid at right angles* to the axis of rotation symmetry*. The part below the cross section is the **frustrum**.

The cross section of a rectangular pyramid is a rectangle.

Frustrum

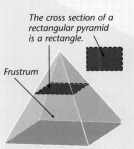

Net

A plane (flat) shape composed of polygons*, which represents the **faces** of a **polyhedron**, and can be folded up to make a polyhedron.

Net of a square-based pyramid

SYMMETRY

A shape has **symmetry** when it can be halved or turned in such a way that it fits exactly onto itself. A plane (flat shape) or solid that is not symmetric is **asymmetric**. There are two types of symmetry: reflection and rotation.

Reflection symmetry, reflective symmetry or line symmetry

Symmetry in which a shape can be divided into two parts by a line or plane, such that each part of the shape is a mirror image of the other.

This butterfly shape has reflection symmetry, as each half is a mirror image of the other.

This bowl has reflection symmetry, as each half is a mirror image of the other.

Line of symmetry or mirror line

A line that divides a plane into two parts, such that each part is a mirror image of the other. A plane can have more than one line of symmetry.

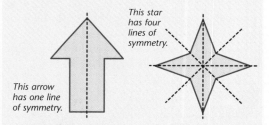

This arrow has one line of symmetry.

This star has four lines of symmetry.

Plane of symmetry

A plane that divides a solid into two parts, such that each part is a mirror image of the other. A solid can have more than one plane of symmetry.

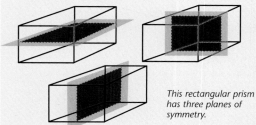

This rectangular prism has three planes of symmetry.

Rotation symmetry or rotational symmetry

Symmetry in which a shape can be turned about a fixed point* or line and fit exactly onto itself.

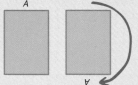

This rectangle has rotation symmetry.

Order of rotation(al) symmetry

The number of times within a revolution (360°) that a shape can be turned to fit exactly onto itself.

This four-pointed star has rotation symmetry of order 4 because it can fit onto itself in 4 different positions.

Center of rotation(al) symmetry

The point* around which a plane can be rotated to fit exactly onto itself.

The dot marks the center of rotation symmetry of this eight-pointed star.

Axis of rotation(al) symmetry

The line around which a solid can be rotated to fit exactly onto itself.

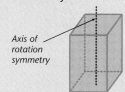

Axis of rotation symmetry

This rectangular prism has rotation symmetry of order 4 about this axis.

** **Perpendicular bisector** 48; **Point** 30; **Vector** 45.*

TRANSFORMATION

In geometry, a **transformation** can change the position, size or shape of a line, plane (flat shape) or solid. The line, plane or solid that is to undergo transformation is called the **object** and the result is the **image**. Performing a transformation is known as **mapping** an object to its image. The points on a mapped image are identified by ', for example, line AB maps to A'B'.

Translation

A transformation in which an object is moved to a new position without being turned or reflected. The translated image is the same size and shape as the object. The change in position from a given point in a given direction is called its **displacement**. During translation, every point is displaced by an equal amount, which can be described by a vector*.

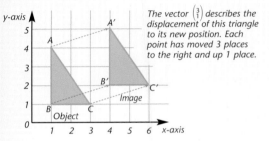

The vector $\binom{3}{1}$ describes the displacement of this triangle to its new position. Each point has moved 3 places to the right and up 1 place.

Reflection

A transformation in which each point is mapped to a corresponding point, which is an equal distance from, and at right angles (90°) to, a **mirror line**. If the object is a plane, the mirror line is a line. If the object is a solid, the mirror line is a plane. The size and angles of the reflected image stay the same as the object, but its **sense** has changed, which means that the image is back to front.

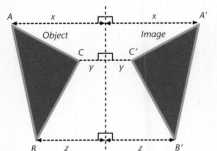

The reflected image is exactly the same shape and size as, but an exact opposite of, the original object. The distances x, y and z are the same on each side of the mirror line.

Rotation

A transformation in which an object is turned so that each point on the image remains the same distance from a fixed point (**center of rotation**) or line (**axis of rotation**), depending whether the object is a plane or a solid. The size and angles of the reflected image are the same as the object, but the image itself is in a different position and at a different angle.

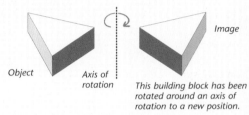

This building block has been rotated around an axis of rotation to a new position.

The center of rotation may be inside, on the edge of, or outside the object. To find the center of rotation, join any two points on the object to their corresponding points on the image, and construct the perpendicular bisector* of each line. The center of rotation lies where the perpendicular bisectors meet.

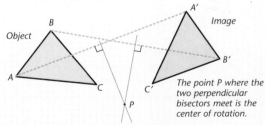

The point P where the two perpendicular bisectors meet is the center of rotation.

The angle through which an object has been turned is called the **angle of rotation**. If the angle of rotation is in a counter-clockwise direction, it is said to be **positive**. If it is clockwise, it is said to be **negative**.

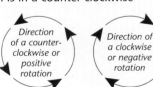

Direction of a counter-clockwise or positive rotation

Direction of a clockwise or negative rotation

Enlargement

A transformation that changes the size but not the shape of an object. An enlargement is measured from a point, called the **center of enlargement**, which can be inside, on the edge of, or outside the object. The amount by which an object is enlarged is called its **scale factor** or **linear scale factor**.

In this example, the image is three times larger than the object, so the scale factor of the enlargement is 3.

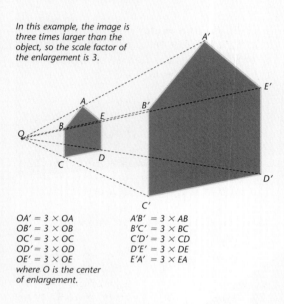

$OA' = 3 \times OA$
$OB' = 3 \times OB$
$OC' = 3 \times OC$
$OD' = 3 \times OD$
$OE' = 3 \times OE$
where O is the center of enlargement.

$A'B' = 3 \times AB$
$B'C' = 3 \times BC$
$C'D' = 3 \times CD$
$D'E' = 3 \times DE$
$E'A' = 3 \times EA$

If a **negative scale factor** is used, the center of enlargement is between the object and the image.

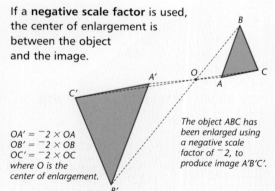

$OA' = {}^-2 \times OA$
$OB' = {}^-2 \times OB$
$OC' = {}^-2 \times OC$
where O is the center of enlargement.

The object ABC has been enlarged using a negative scale factor of $^-2$, to produce image A'B'C'.

A **fractional scale factor** is between $^-1$ and 1. It results in an image that is smaller than the object.

Image A'B'C' is the result of applying a scale factor of $\frac{1}{2}$ to object ABC.

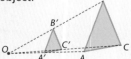

Glide reflection

A transformation in which an object undergoes translation*, and is then reflected* in a mirror line* that is parallel* to the translation. The size and angles of the image are the same as the object, but the image is back to front and displaced.

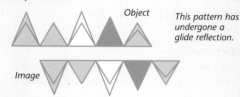

This pattern has undergone a glide reflection.

Similar figures

Objects that are the same shape but different sizes, such as those produced by **enlargement**.

These figures are similar: they are the same shape but different sizes.

Congruent figures

Objects that are exactly the same shape and size, including those that are a mirror image of each other. Reflection*, translation* and rotation* produce congruent figures.

These three figures are congruent: they are all the same shape and size.

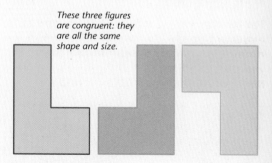

Invariance property

A property of an object that remains unchanged by transformation. For example, the shape of an object in translation*, reflection*, rotation* or **enlargement** is invariant because it does not change.

* **Mirror line** 43 (**Reflection**); **Parallel** 30; **Pythagorean theorem** 38; **Reflection** 43; **Right-angled triangle** 37; **Rotation**, **Translation** 43.

VECTORS

A **vector** is a quantity that has both **magnitude** (size) and direction. **Displacement** (change in position) is one example of a vector quantity. It is used on these pages to show the basic properties of vectors, which can be applied to all vector quantities.

Displacement is the distance an object has moved in a particular direction, for example the displacement of B from A is 3km northeast.

Vector notation

The ways in which vectors are represented. A vector can be drawn as a **directed line**, that is, a line with an arrow on it. The line shows the magnitude of the vector and the arrow indicates its direction.

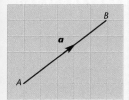

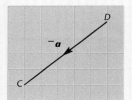

This vector can be written as **AB** or $\overrightarrow{AB}$. It can also be written as **a** (in print), and $\underline{a}$ or $\underset{\sim}{a}$ (if it is handwritten).

This vector can be written as **DC** or $\overrightarrow{DC}$. It can also be written as ⁻**a** (in print), and $-\underline{a}$ or $-\underset{\sim}{a}$ (if it is handwritten).

A vector can also be written as a **column vector**, in the form $\begin{pmatrix} x \\ y \end{pmatrix}$.

The top number in a column vector represents movement parallel* to the x-axis. The bottom number represents movement parallel to the y-axis. Movement up and to the right is positive. Movement down and to the left is negative.

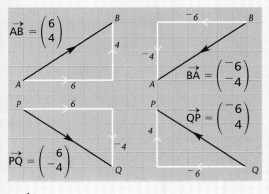

$$\overrightarrow{AB} = \begin{pmatrix} 6 \\ 4 \end{pmatrix}$$

$$\overrightarrow{BA} = \begin{pmatrix} -6 \\ -4 \end{pmatrix}$$

$$\overrightarrow{QP} = \begin{pmatrix} -6 \\ 4 \end{pmatrix}$$

$$\overrightarrow{PQ} = \begin{pmatrix} 6 \\ -4 \end{pmatrix}$$

Magnitude of a vector

The size of a vector. For example, the magnitude of displacement is the distance an object has moved. The magnitude of **a** is written | **a** |.

The length of a vector gives its magnitude. To find the length of a vector, draw the distance moved along the x-axis and y-axis, so forming a right-angled triangle* which has the vector as the hypotenuse (the longest side). Then use the Pythagorean theorem* ($a^2 + b^2 = c^2$) to find the length of the hypotenuse.

For example, to find the magnitude of **x**:

$$|x| = \sqrt{a^2 + b^2}$$
$$|x| = \sqrt{3^2 + 4^2}$$
$$|x| = \sqrt{9 + 16}$$
$$|x| = \sqrt{25}$$
$$|x| = 5$$

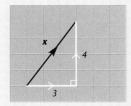

Equal vectors

Vectors that have the same magnitude and direction.

*Vectors **x** and **y** are equal: they have the same length and direction (that is, they are parallel*).*

*Vectors **p** and **q** are not equal. They are the same length but do not have the same direction.*

A parallel vector with the same magnitude as **m** but the opposite direction is called ⁻**m**. The two vectors are not equal.*

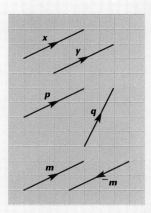

Arithmetic with vectors

To add or subtract vectors

Draw the first vector, then draw the second vector at the end of it. Join the ends of the vectors to create a third vector, called the **resultant**. This represents the combined change along the x-axis, and the combined change along the y-axis.

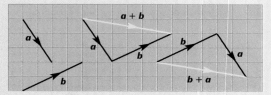

To add vectors, join them with the arrows pointing the same way (both clockwise* or counter-clockwise*). Vectors obey the commutative* and associative laws* of addition, as the resultant $a + b = b + a$.

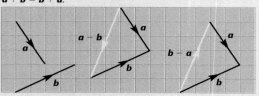

To subtract vectors, join them with the arrows pointing the opposite way (one clockwise*, the other counter-clockwise*).

To find the resultant of two column vectors*, add or subtract the top number in each vector (the change along the x-axis), then add or subtract the bottom number in each vector (the change along the y-axis).
e.g.

$$a + b = \begin{pmatrix} 2 \\ -3 \end{pmatrix} + \begin{pmatrix} 4 \\ 2 \end{pmatrix} = \begin{pmatrix} 6 \\ -1 \end{pmatrix}$$

$$b + a = \begin{pmatrix} 4 \\ 2 \end{pmatrix} + \begin{pmatrix} 2 \\ -3 \end{pmatrix} = \begin{pmatrix} 6 \\ -1 \end{pmatrix}$$

$$a - b = \begin{pmatrix} 2 \\ -3 \end{pmatrix} - \begin{pmatrix} 4 \\ 2 \end{pmatrix} = \begin{pmatrix} -2 \\ -5 \end{pmatrix}$$

$$b - a = \begin{pmatrix} 4 \\ 2 \end{pmatrix} - \begin{pmatrix} 2 \\ -3 \end{pmatrix} = \begin{pmatrix} 2 \\ 5 \end{pmatrix}$$

Scalar or scalar quantity

A quantity that has magnitude*, but no direction. Speed* is a scalar quantity, as it has size (distance per unit of time) but no direction.

To multiply a vector by a scalar

Write the vector as a column vector* and multiply each number in the vector by the **scalar**.
e.g.

$$2 \times \begin{pmatrix} 4 \\ 2 \end{pmatrix} = \begin{pmatrix} 8 \\ 4 \end{pmatrix}$$

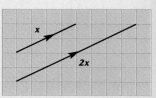

This diagram shows vectors x and $2x$, as expressed in the column vectors above.

Multiplying a vector by a scalar is sometimes called **scalar multiplication**. A vector cannot be multiplied by another vector.

Geometry with vectors

Vectors can be applied to geometrical problems. For example, the shape below is formed from a series of vectors. By finding an expression for each vector, you can learn about the relative lengths of the sides.

For example, in the diagram below, point B is the midpoint* of $\overrightarrow{AX}$. Find expressions for the vectors $\overrightarrow{YB}$, $\overrightarrow{AB}$, $\overrightarrow{YA}$ and $\overrightarrow{AZ}$.

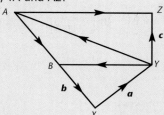

$\overrightarrow{YB} = \overrightarrow{YX} + \overrightarrow{XB} = {}^-a + {}^-b = {}^-a - b$
This is because the direction of a and b need to be reversed to get from point Y to point B.

$\overrightarrow{AB} = \overrightarrow{BX} = b$
This is because B is the midpoint of $\overrightarrow{AX}$, and $\overrightarrow{BX}$ is b.

$\overrightarrow{YA} = \overrightarrow{YB} + \overrightarrow{BA} = ({}^-a - b) + {}^-b$
$= {}^-a - b - b = {}^-a - 2b$
This is because $\overrightarrow{YB} = {}^-a - b$ (see above) and $\overrightarrow{BA}$ is the reverse of $\overrightarrow{AB}$, so is ^-b.

$\overrightarrow{AZ} = \overrightarrow{AY} + \overrightarrow{YZ} = a + 2b + c$
This is because $\overrightarrow{AY}$ is the reverse of $\overrightarrow{YA}$.
$\overrightarrow{YA} = {}^-a - 2b$, so $\overrightarrow{AY}$ is $a + 2b$.

GEOMETRIC CONSTRUCTIONS

Construction is the process of drawing geometric figures. Some figures can be constructed using only compasses and a ruler; others need a protractor too.

Compasses or a pair of compasses

A mathematical instrument used for drawing circles* and arcs*. They can also be used to transfer distances from a ruler to paper, or from one part of a drawing to another. Compasses have two legs which are joined at one end. One leg holds a pencil or lead, the other is a sharp point, which serves as a fixed pivot.

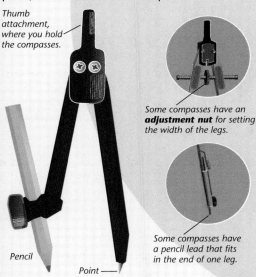

Thumb attachment, where you hold the compasses.

*Some compasses have an **adjustment nut** for setting the width of the legs.*

Pencil

Point

Some compasses have a pencil lead that fits in the end of one leg.

To draw an arc or circle with compasses

Hold the thumb attachment with the thumb and first finger. Swing the compasses in a clockwise* direction and draw the arc* or circle*, keeping equal pressure on both legs of the compasses.

To help to prevent the legs from slipping, tilt the compasses in the direction in which they are being rotated.

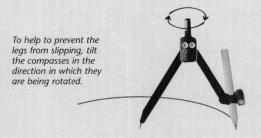

Using compasses

Before starting, close the compasses and make sure that the tip of the compass point touches the end of the pencil lead. To set the compasses, hold them with the point in the zero marking on the ruler. Pull the other leg out (or turn the adjustment nut) until the pencil lead rests on the required ruler marking.

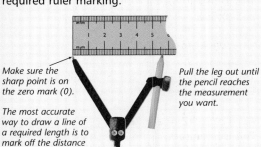

Make sure the sharp point is on the zero mark (0).

Pull the leg out until the pencil reaches the measurement you want.

The most accurate way to draw a line of a required length is to mark off the distance using compasses.

Protractor

An instrument used for measuring or drawing angles on paper. A protractor is usually a flat transparent semicircle or circle, with degrees marked around the edge. When measuring an angle with a protractor, always read the scale starting from zero.

Angle a is measured on the outside scale of the protractor, to give an angle of 45°.

Angle b is measured on the inside scale, to give an angle of 77°.

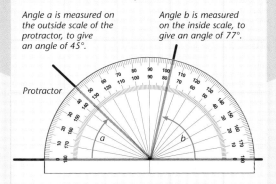

Protractor

To find the size of a reflex* angle, first measure its adjacent angle*, which is less than 180°, and subtract this from 360°.

To find angle a, measure angle b and subtract it from 360°.

e.g. if angle b = 85°
360° − 85° = 275°
so, angle a = 275°

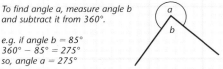

Internet links For links to useful websites on **geometric constructions**, go to *www.usborne-quicklinks.com*

Useful construction terms

Midpoint
A point* that is exactly half way along a line segment*.

Point P is the midpoint of line AB.

Intersection
A point* where two or more lines cross each other.

Point P is the intersection of lines AB and CD.

Equidistant
The term that describes two or more points*, lines or solids that are the same distance away from another point, line or solid.

Points A, B, C, D, E and F are equidistant from P.

Bisector
A line that cuts an angle* exactly in half.

Perpendicular bisector
A bisector that is at right angles* to the line it halves.

Basic constructions

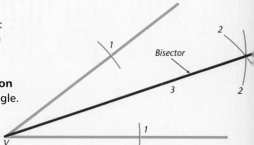

To bisect an angle
To bisect the angle* shown in the diagram on the right:
1. Place the point of the compasses* on the vertex* (V) and draw an arc* on each arm* of the angle*.

2. Place the point of the compasses on each **intersection** in turn and draw an arc between the arms of the angle.

3. Draw a straight line from the intersection of these arcs to the vertex. The resulting line is the **bisector**.

To construct a perpendicular bisector
To construct a **perpendicular bisector** on the line segment AB below:
1. Set a pair of compasses* to slightly more than half the length of the line. Place the point at A and draw an arc* on each side.

2. Without changing the setting of the compasses, place the point at B and draw another arc on each side.

3. Join both points where the arcs meet to find the perpendicular bisector.

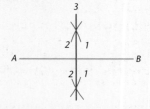

To construct a perpendicular line through a particular point
To construct a line perpendicular* to the segment AB shown below, through point P:
1. Place the point of the compasses at P and draw arcs that intersect AB.

2. Place the compasses on each intersection in turn and draw an arc on the opposite side of the line to P.

3. Join P with the point where these arcs intersect. The line that you have drawn will be perpendicular to the line AB.

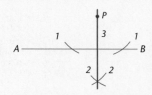

* **Angle** 32; **Arc** 47 (**To draw an arc...**); **Arm** 32 (Introduction); **Compasses** 47; **Included angle** 37 (**Angles in a triangle**); **Line segment** 30; **Perpendicular, Point** 30; **Protractor** 47; **Right angle** 32; **Vertex** 34 (**Polygons**).

Constructing triangles

To construct a triangle when all three sides are known

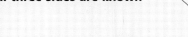   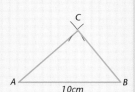

1. Draw a line of the longest known length. Label the ends.

2. Set the compasses* to the second length. Place the point of the compasses at A and draw an arc*.

3. Set the compasses to the third length, place the point at B and draw another arc. Label the **intersection**.

4. Join A and B to the intersection.
(To construct an equilateral triangle, keep the compasses set to the same length as AB.)

To construct a triangle when two angles and a side are known

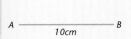  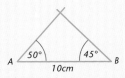 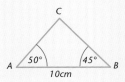

1. Draw a line the length of the known side, and label the ends.

2. Measure the first angle* at A with a protractor* and mark it in. Extend the arm* of the angle.

3. Measure the second angle from B and mark it in. Extend the arm of the angle.

4. Label the point where the two lines intersect.

To construct a triangle when two sides and the included angle are known

 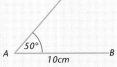 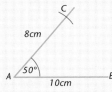 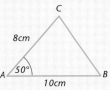

1. Draw a line the length of the longest known side, and label the ends.

2. Measure the included angle* at A with a protractor and mark it in. Extend the arm* of the angle.

3. Set the compasses* to the length of the second arc, place the point at A and draw an arc* on the extended arm. Label the point where the lines intersect.

4. Complete the triangle by joining C and B.

Triangles with two solutions

If the information given about a triangle is not enough to enable you to construct it, it can have two possible solutions. This is called the **ambiguous case**.

For example, to construct the triangle where side AB = 7.5cm, side AC = 5cm and angle* ABC = 50°:

  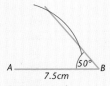 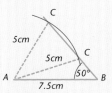

1. Draw side AB and label the ends.

2. Using a protractor*, measure the angle ABC at B and extend the arm* of the angle.

3. Set a pair of compasses* to the length of side AC and draw a wide arc* from point A.

4. The two points where the arc intersects the line provide the two possible solutions to the triangle.

Internet links For links to useful websites on **geometric constructions**, go to www.usborne-quicklinks.com

Other constructions

To construct a regular polygon*

For example, to construct a regular pentagon*, divide the sum of the interior angles* (540°) by the number of angles* in a pentagon (5), to give the size of each angle (108°).

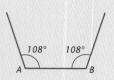
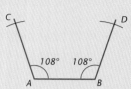
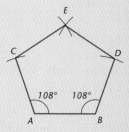

1. Draw a line to form the base of the pentagon. Label the ends A and B.

2. Use a protractor* to measure the required angles at A and B. Extend the arms* of the angles.

3. Set a pair of compasses* to the length of the base. Position the point at A and B in turn and draw an arc* at the arm of each angle. Label the intersections* C and D.

4. Place the point of the compasses at C and D in turn and draw two more arcs. Label the point where the arcs cross (E). Join C and D to E to finish the pentagon.

To draw a diagram of a straight-sided solid

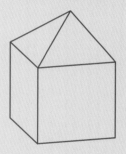
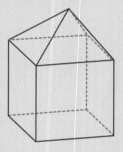
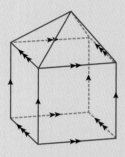
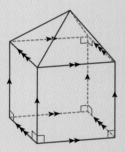

1. Draw the edges you can see. Make sure that you draw vertical* lines vertically.

2. Show edges that cannot be seen as dotted lines.

3. Mark parallel* lines. If there is more than one set, use different marks for each set.

4. Mark 90° angles on the diagram as right angles*. It is particularly important to do this where angles do not look as if they are 90°.

Isometric paper

Paper printed with three sets of parallel* lines, each set being at 60° angles to the other sets. Using isometric paper makes it easier to draw an object and give the effect that it is three-dimensional*.

When using isometric paper, always make sure that one set of lines is placed vertically, as shown below.*

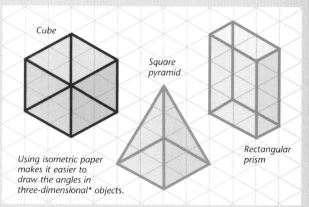

Cube

Square pyramid

Rectangular prism

Using isometric paper makes it easier to draw the angles in three-dimensional* objects.

* **Angle** 32; **Arc** 47 (**To draw an arc**); **Arm** 32 (Introduction); **Bisector** 48; **Compasses** 47; **Interior angle** 34; **Intersection** 48; **Line segment, Parallel** 30; **Pentagon** 34 (**Regular polygon**); **Perpendicular bisector** 48; **Point** 30; **Protractor** 47; **Radius** 65; **Regular polygon** 35; **Right angle** 32; **Semicircle** 65; **Three-dimensional** 31 (**Dimensions**); **Vertical** 30.

LOCI

Loci is the plural of locus. A **locus** is a set of points* that satisfy a particular condition, and it can be a path or a region. For example, if you stand with your arms stretched out to the side and turn around in one place, the locus of your fingertips is a circular path. Your body is at the center of the circle and the circle's radius* is the length of your arm.

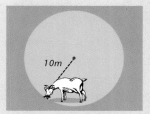

This goat is tethered by a 10m rope to a post in a field. If it can eat any grass within reach, the locus of the goat is a circular region of radius 10m and with the post at the center.*

Locus from a fixed point

The locus of a point* that is the same distance from a fixed point is a circle.

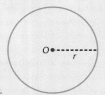

The locus of a point that is always at a distance r from a fixed point O is a circle. The center of the circle is O and its radius is r.

Locus from two fixed points

The locus of a point* that is the same distance from two fixed points is the perpendicular bisector* of the line drawn between the points.

Any point on the locus is the same distance from points P and Q.

Locus from a line

The locus of a point* that is the same distance *d* from a line is two parallel* lines, one each side of the original line at a distance *d* from it.

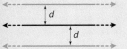

The locus of each line is as long as the line.

The locus of a line segment is two parallel* lines, and two semicircles*.*

Locus from intersecting lines

The locus of a point* that is the same distance from two intersecting lines is the bisector* of the angle* between those lines.

Any point on the locus is the same distance from OA as it is from OB.

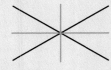

The bisectors (shown here in blue) of a pair of intersecting lines are always at right angles to each other.*

Compound loci

A set of points* that satisfy more than one condition. When drawing compound loci:

1. Draw a sketch of what you think the locus will look like.

2. Use a ruler and compasses* to construct your final diagram. Do not erase the construction lines you have drawn.

3. Add any necessary labels but keep your diagram as clear and simple as you can.

4. Shade the part of the diagram that satisfies all conditions and state what the area represents. Use a solid line to show a boundary that is included in the condition, and a dotted line to show one that is not.

For example, the points P and Q are 3cm apart. Find the set of points that are less than 2cm from P but are closer to Q than P.

1. Sketch the loci. To find the points that are less than 2cm from P, draw a circle of radius 2cm. To find which points are closer to Q than P, draw the perpendicular bisector* of PQ.*

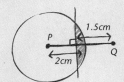

2. Construct the loci. Here, the perpendicular bisector is a dotted line. Points on it are not included in the condition: they are the same distance from P and Q, and so are not closer to Q.

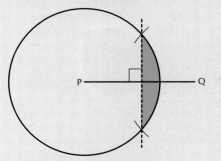

The shaded region is the set of points that are less than 2cm from P but are closer to Q than P.

DRAWING TO SCALE

Many objects are too big or too small to draw the same size as they really are. In a **scale drawing**, each length of an object is increased or decreased in a given ratio*. The finished drawing is larger or smaller than the original object, but the relationships between all the lengths in the object stay the same.

This is a scale drawing of the Eiffel Tower, in Paris, France. The real Eiffel Tower is 70,000 times bigger.

Size

Scale

A fixed ratio that represents the relationship between a drawing (or model) and the real object. The scale is usually written as *x : y*, where *x* represents the measurement used on the reproduction and *y* is the corresponding measurement on the real object.

For example, a scale of 1 : 1000 means that one unit of length on the scale drawing represents 1000 units of the real object.

Scale up

To increase proportionately* in size. An object that has been scaled up will have a scale in which the first figure is larger than the second.

This star has been scaled up.

e.g.
Scale = 3 : 1

3cm

2cm

On this scale drawing of a lady bug, 3cm represent 1cm. What is the real size of the lady bug, to the nearest mm?

3cm represents 3 ÷ 3cm
= 1cm = 10mm

2cm represents 2 ÷ 3cm
= 0.66cm = 7mm (to nearest mm)

The lady bug is 10mm long and 7mm wide.

Scale down

To decrease proportionately* in size. An object that has been scaled down will have a scale in which the first figure is smaller than the second.

This star has been scaled down.

e.g.   *Scale = 1 : 2,750*

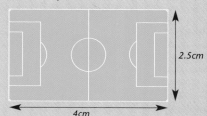

2.5cm

4cm

On this scale drawing of a soccer field, 1cm represents 2,750cm. What is the real size of the field, to the nearest 10m?

4cm represents 4 × 2,750cm
= 11,000cm = 110m

2.5cm represents 2.5 × 2,750cm
= 6,875cm = 68.75m = 70m (to nearest 10m)

The soccer field is 110m long and 70m wide.

Scale factor

The amount by which an object has been reduced or enlarged. For example, if an object has been drawn 10 times larger, the scale factor is 10. If it has been drawn at half its size, the scale factor is $\frac{1}{2}$. To find the scale factor, use:

$$\text{scale factor} = \frac{\text{length on scale drawing}}{\text{length on original object}}$$

(See also *Enlargement* on page 44.)

* **Angle** 32; **Clockwise** 32; **Horizontal** 30; **Proportion** 25; **Ratio** 24.

Direction

Compass

An instrument for finding direction. A compass has a magnetized needle that swings freely on a pivot so it points to north. The four main points on a compass are north (N) at the top, south (S) at the bottom, east (E) at the right and west (W) at the left. Between these are a second set of points: northeast (NE), southeast (SE), southwest (SW) and northwest (NW).

This picture shows the position of eight compass points. The markings on the inner circle show degrees.

North is often indicated on a drawing by an arrow. Once you know which way is north, you can work out other directions.

A is west of B and C is south of B. B is east of A and north of C.

If a direction falls between the compass points, it is measured in degrees from the north or south, whichever is the nearer.

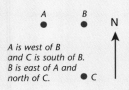

The direction of P from O is N60°E.

The direction of B from A is S40°W.

By using a combination of **scale** and compass points you can make drawings, such as maps, which accurately reflect distance and direction.

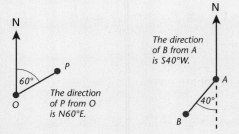

This map shows that Anytown is 20km north of Hereby and 35km northwest of Thereby.

Scale = 1 : 1,000,000

Three-figure bearings

A common method of describing the direction of one point in relation to another. Three-figure bearings are measured clockwise* from the north. To find the bearing of Q from P, start at P looking north and turn in a clockwise direction (to the right) until you are facing Q.

For example, the three-figure bearing of point Q from point P is 285°.

If the angle turned through is less than 100°, place a zero in front of the measurement to give a three-figure bearing.

For example, the bearing of point R from point P is 060°.

Angle of elevation

The angle* through which your line of sight is raised above the horizontal* in order to look at an object.

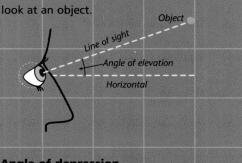

Angle of depression

The angle* through which your line of sight is lowered below the horizontal* in order to look at an object.

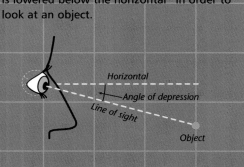

Making a scale drawing

To make a scale drawing

1. Make a sketch of the object. This will give you a rough idea of what your final drawing should look like. Mark all given angles* and full-size dimensions on the sketch.

2. Choose a suitable scale* for your drawing.

3. Make a second sketch, and mark on it the scaled measurements, as well as all angles you need to make your final drawing.

4. Construct the final, accurate drawing, using the measurements you have calculated.

5. Mark the scale on your drawing. If appropriate, give your drawing a title.

6. Find any unknown measurements by measuring the distance (to the nearest millimeter) with compasses* and a ruler and multiplying by the scale factor*.

Example

During a refurbishment of a sports center, a rectangular swimming pool has a shallow children's pool built onto one end. The original pool measures 10m by 20m. The children's pool is shaped like half a regular hexagon and the length of each side of the hexagon is 5m.

Using a scale of 1cm to 2.5m, make a scale drawing of the new pool. Use your drawing to find, to the nearest tenth of a meter, the total length of the new pool.

Scale 1cm : 2.5m

New swimming pool

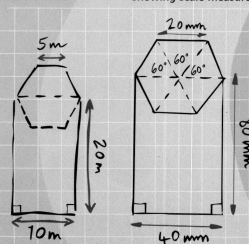

Sketch showing actual measurements

More accurate sketch showing scale measurements

A is the midpoint of the edge of the children's pool and B is the midpoint of the edge of the original pool. From the drawing, AB measures 97mm, so the total length of the new pool is 24.3m (to the nearest tenth of a meter).

* **Angle** 32; **Compasses** 47; **Diameter** 65; **Pi** 66; **Polygon** 34; **Scale, Scale factor** 52; **Sum** 14 (**Addition**); **Two-dimensional** 31 (**Dimensions**).

PERIMETER AND AREA

The distance around the edge of a shape is its **perimeter**. The amount of space occupied by a two-dimensional* shape is its **area**. The area of a shape is usually measured in **square units**: square millimeters (mm²) and square centimeters (cm²) for smaller areas, and square meters (m²) and square kilometers (km²) for large areas. Very large areas, such as farmland, can be measured in acres. One acre is equal to 4,047m² (or 4,840yd²).

Perimeter

To find the perimeter of a straight-sided shape, add together the lengths of all the sides.

Perimeter = total distance around the edge

Perimeter = sum* of all sides

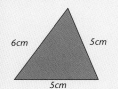

6cm   5cm

5cm

For example, the perimeter of this triangle is:

6 + 5 + 5 = 16cm

The perimeter of a circle is called the **circumference**. To find the circumference of a circle, multiply pi* by the diameter* of the circle. Pi is equal to approximately 3.14, or you can leave your answer in terms of pi. The symbol for pi is the Greek letter π.

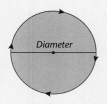

The edge of a circle is its circumference. The diameter is the distance across the center.

Diameter

The formula for calculating the circumference of a circle is:

circumference = π × d (or πd)

where *d* is the diameter.

For example, the circumference of this circle is:

π × d

= π × 5.5

= 5.5πcm

or

5.5 × 3.14

= 17.27cm

5.5cm

Area

Estimating area

To estimate the area of a shape, draw it on a piece of squared paper and count the number of squares it covers.

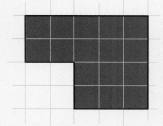

The area of this shape is 16 square units.

If a polygon* does not fit exactly on the grid lines, count the whole squares inside it, then count how many whole squares can be made up from the parts.

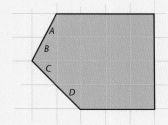

A
B
C
D

This shape covers 15 whole squares. A and B fit together to make a square, as do C and D. The area of this shape is 17 square units (15 + 2).

If a shape hardly fits the grid lines at all, estimate its area by counting as one square any part of the shape that covers half a square or more. Ignore any part of the shape that covers less than half a square.

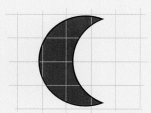

The area of this shape is approximately 4 square units.

Internet links For links to useful websites on **area and volume**, go to *www.usborne-quicklinks.com*

Area formulas

The area of many shapes can be calculated using rules or formulas*. These rules can then be applied to a shape of any size.

Area of a rectangle

To find the area of a rectangle*, count or measure the number of units in its length and multiply this by the number of units in its width.

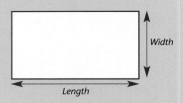

Width

Length

The rule for finding the area of a rectangle is:
area = length × width
This can be expressed by the formula* $a = l \times w$

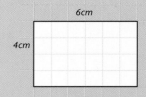

6cm

4cm

For example, the area of this rectangle is:
$6 \times 4 = 24\text{cm}^2$

Area of a square

Like the area of a rectangle*, the area of a square* is found by multiplying its length and width.

As the length and the width are the same though, the area can be shown by the rule:
area = (side)²

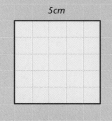

5cm

For example, the area of this square is:
$5 \times 5 = 25\text{cm}^2$

Area of a triangle

To find the area of a triangle*, you need to know its **perpendicular height**. The perpendicular height is a line from the apex* of the triangle that meets the base at right angles (90°). Any side of the triangle can be the base.

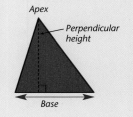

Apex

Perpendicular height

In many triangles, the perpendicular height is within the triangle.

Base

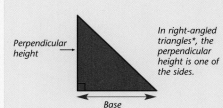

Perpendicular height

In right-angled triangles*, the perpendicular height is one of the sides.

Base

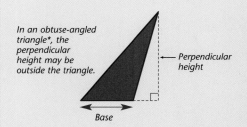

In an obtuse-angled triangle*, the perpendicular height may be outside the triangle.

Perpendicular height

Base

The rule for calculating the area of a triangle is:
area = $\frac{1}{2}$ × (base × perpendicular height)
This can be expressed by the formula* $a = \frac{1}{2}bh$.

This rule is sometimes written:
$$\text{area} = \frac{\text{base} \times \text{perpendicular height}}{2}$$

For example, the area of this triangle is:
$\frac{1}{2} \times (5 \times 6)$
$= \frac{1}{2} \times 30$
$= 15\text{cm}^2$

5cm

6cm

* **Apex** 37 (**Angles in a triangle**); **Circles** 65; **Formula** 75; **Obtuse-angled triangle** 37; **Parallel** 30; **Parallelogram** 39;
Pi 66; **Polyhedron** 40; **Radius** 65; **Rectangle** 39; **Right-angled triangle** 37; **Square** 39;
Sum 14 (**Addition**); **Trapezoid** 39; **Triangle** 37; **Vertex** 34.

Area of a parallelogram

To find the area of a parallelogram*, you need to know its **perpendicular height** (a line from a vertex* that meets the base at right angles (90°)).

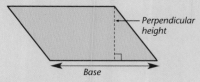

Perpendicular height

Base

The rule for calculating the area of a parallelogram is:

area = base × perpendicular height

This can be expressed by the formula* $a = bh$.

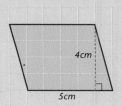

4cm

5cm

For example, the area of this parallelogram is:
$4 \times 5 = 20\text{cm}^2$

Area of a trapezoid

To find the area of a trapezoid*, you need to know the length of the parallel* sides (a and b) and the distance between them (h).

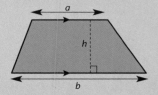

a

h

b

The formula* for calculating the area of a trapezoid is:

$$\text{area} = \frac{1}{2} \times (a + b) \times h$$

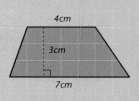

4cm

3cm

7cm

For example, the area of this trapezoid is:

$\frac{1}{2} \times (4 + 7) \times 3$

$= \frac{1}{2} \times 11 \times 3$

$= \frac{1}{2} \times 33$

$= 16.5\text{cm}^2$

Area of a circle

To find the area of a circle*, you need to know its radius*. The radius is the distance from the center to any point on the circumference (edge).

Radius

The formula* for calculating the area of a circle is:

area = π × r^2

or **area = π r^2**

where π (Pi*) is equal to approximately 3.14 and r is the radius.

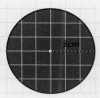

3cm

For example, the area of this circle is:

$\pi \times 3^2$

$= 3.14 \times 9$

$= 28.3\text{cm}^2$ (3 s.f.)

Surface area

The sum* of the areas of all surfaces of a solid is called its **surface area**.

The rule for calculating the surface area of any solid is:

surface area = sum of area of surfaces

For example, this prism has 3 equal rectangular faces and 2 equal triangular faces. So, the surface area of this prism is calculated as:

$3(5 \times 3) + 2 (\frac{1}{2} \times 3 \times 2)$

$= 45 + 6$

$= 51\text{cm}^2$

5cm

2cm

3cm

In general, the rule for calculating the surface area of a regular polyhedron* is:

**surface area =
area of side × number of sides**

4cm

4cm   4cm

The surface area of this cube is:

$6 \times (4 \times 4)$

$= 96\text{cm}^2$

VOLUME

The amount of solid occupied by a three-dimensional* shape is called its **volume**. This space can be measured by the number of **unit cubes** that can fit inside it. Common units of measuring volume are based on the units of length, for example, cubic centimeters (cm³) and cubic meters (m³).

A total of 36 cubes would be needed to fill the space taken up by the rectangular prism below (3 layers with 4 × 3 cubes on each layer). This can be written as: volume of rectangular prism = 3 × 4 × 3 = 36 cubic units

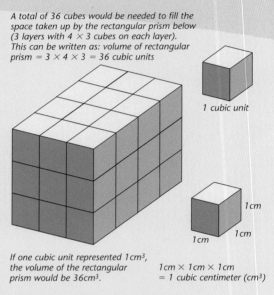

1 cubic unit

1cm

1cm

1cm

If one cubic unit represented 1cm³, the volume of the rectangular prism would be 36cm³.

1cm × 1cm × 1cm = 1 cubic centimeter (cm³)

Volume formulas

The volume of many solids can be calculated using rules or formulas*. These rules can be applied to a solid of any size.

The formula for finding the volume of a solid often contains the formula for finding the area* of its base. This is because a three-dimensional shape can be thought of as lots of layers, as in the rectangular prism example above.

In some solids, such as a cylinder, the area of each layer is the same size. This is called a **uniform cross section**. In others, like a cone, the area of a cross section* varies throughout the shape.

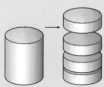
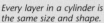

Every layer in a cylinder is the same size and shape.

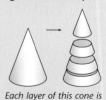

Each layer of this cone is a different size and shape.

Volume of a rectangular prism

The volume of a rectangular prism* is calculated using: **volume = length × width × height**

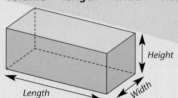

Height

Length

Width

For example, the volume of a rectangular prism of length 8cm, width 3cm and height 4cm is:

$8 \times 3 \times 4$
$= 96\text{cm}^3$

Volume of a prism

The volume of a prism* is calculated using:
volume = area of cross section × height

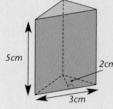

5cm

2cm

3cm

The formula* for calculating the area of the cross section* will depend on the shape of the base (see pages 56–57).

This prism has a triangular base, so you will need to use the formula for the area of a triangle:
area = $\frac{1}{2}$ × (base × perpendicular height)
The volume of this prism is therefore:
$(\frac{1}{2} \times 3 \times 2) \times 5$
$= 5\text{cm}^3$

A cylinder has a circular base, so the volume is calculated by multiplying the area of the circle by the height of the cylinder:
volume = πr^2 × height

For example, the volume of this cylinder is:

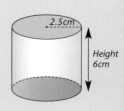

2.5cm

Height 6cm

$\pi \times (2.5)^2 \times 6$
$= \pi \times 6.25 \times 6$
$= 117.75\text{cm}^3$
$= 118\text{cm}^3 \text{ (3 s.f.)}$

* **Area** 55; **Cone** 41; **Cross section** 41; **Formula** 75; **Mass** 72; **Prism** 41; **Pyramid** 68; **Radius** 65; **Rectangular prism** 41; **Three-dimensional** 31 (**Dimensions**).

Volume of a pyramid or cone

The volume of a cone* or pyramid* is calculated using the formula*:

volume = $\frac{1}{3}$ × area of base × height

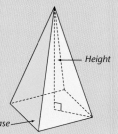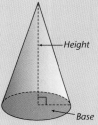

Height

Height

Base

Base

For example, the volume of this square-based pyramid is:

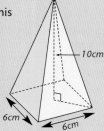

10cm

6cm

6cm

$\frac{1}{3} \times (6 \times 6) \times 10$

$= \frac{1}{3} \times 36 \times 10$

$= 120\text{cm}^3$

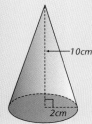

10cm

2cm

The volume of this cone is:

$\frac{1}{3} \times \pi r^2 \times 10$

$= \frac{1}{3} \times (\pi \times 4) \times 10$

$= \frac{1}{3} \times 125.66371$

$= 41.9\text{cm}^3$ (3 s.f.)

Volume of a sphere

The volume of a sphere is calculated using:

volume = $\frac{4}{3} \times \pi \times r^3$

where r is the radius* of the cross section* of the sphere.

r

This sphere has been cut in half to reveal its cross section.

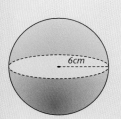

6cm

For example, the volume of this sphere can be calculated using:

$\frac{4}{3} \times \pi \times 6^3$

$= \frac{4}{3} \times \pi \times 216$

$= 904\text{cm}^3$ (3 s.f.)

Volume and capacity

The volume of an object is closely related to its **capacity** – that is, the amount it can contain. Capacity is measured in milliliters (ml) and liters (l).

A container with a volume of 1cm³ holds 1 milliliter of liquid, and a container with a volume of 1,000cm³ holds 1 liter.

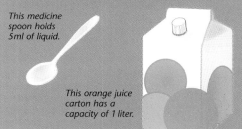

This medicine spoon holds 5ml of liquid.

This orange juice carton has a capacity of 1 liter.

Density

Density is the mass* of one unit volume of a material from which an object is made. This is usually described as "mass per unit volume". Density is measured in grams per cubic centimeter (g/cm³) or kilograms per cubic meter (kg/m³). The rule for calculating density is:

density = $\dfrac{\text{mass}}{\text{volume}}$

For example, find the density of this house brick and bath sponge.

Mass of brick = 2.4kg
Volume of brick = 1,260cm³

Density of brick $= \dfrac{2400\text{g}}{1260\text{cm}^3}$

$= 1.9\text{g/cm}^3$ (2 s.f.)

Mass of sponge = 200g
Volume of sponge = 1,260cm³

Density of sponge $= \dfrac{200\text{g}}{1260\text{cm}^3}$

$= 0.16\text{g/cm}^3$ (2 s.f.)

A comparison of the results shows that brick is a denser material than sponge.

Internet links For links to useful websites on **area and volume**, go to *www.usborne-quicklinks.com*

TRIGONOMETRY

Trigonometry is the branch of mathematics concerned with the relationships between the sides* of triangles* and their angles*. These relationships are described in terms of three main functions* of the angles: **sine**, **cosine** and **tangent**, which are known as **trigonometric** or **circular functions**. In trigonometry, unknown angles are often represented by Greek letters, such as α (*alpha*) and θ (*theta*).

Before you can use sine, cosine and tangent, you need to be able to identify the parts of a right-angled triangle. This diagram shows the parts in relation to angle θ.*

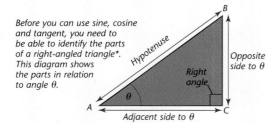

Opposite side (opp)
The side opposite the angle in question. In the diagram above, the side opposite θ is BC.

Adjacent side (adj)
The side next to the angle in question. In the diagram above, the side adjacent to θ is AC.

Hypotenuse (hyp)
The longest side of a right-angled triangle*, opposite the right angle (the 90° angle). In the diagram above, AB is the hypotenuse.

Pythagorean theorem
The theorem which states that in a right-angled triangle*, the square* of the **hypotenuse** is equal to the sum* of the squares of the other two sides. You can read more about the Pythagorean theorem on page 38.

The Pythagorean theorem states that $c^2 = a^2 + b^2$

Finding unknown sides

There are three formulas* that can help you to find the length of an unknown side or angle of a right-angled triangle*. These formulas are called the **sine ratio**, **cosine ratio** and **tangent ratio**.

Sine ratio (sin)
The formula*:

$$\text{sine } \theta = \frac{\text{length of opposite side}}{\text{length of hypotenuse}}$$

Use the sine ratio if you know or need to know the **opposite** side or the **hypotenuse**. For example, to find the length of side *a* of this triangle, substitute the known values into the sine ratio:

$$\sin \theta = \frac{\text{length of opposite side}}{\text{length of hypotenuse}}$$

$$\sin 48° = \frac{a}{9}$$

Rearrange* the formula to solve for *a*:

$$a = 9 \times \sin 48°$$

Use the "sin" button on your calculator to find the value of sin 48°, and so solve the equation*:

$$a = 9 \times 0.743\,144\,82$$
$$a = 6.69\text{cm (2 d.p.)}$$

Side *a* is 6.69cm long (to 2 d.p.).

Using your calculator

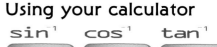

*The keys for sine, cosine and tangent can be found on a scientific calculator, usually labeled **sin**, **cos** and **tan**.*

On some calculators, the **sine**, **cosine** and **tangent** buttons are used to find the inverse (opposite) of these functions (shown above each button), but you will probably need to press a "shift" or "inverse" key first. Calculators can work in different units, so make sure your calculator is in "DEG" mode, so it gives angles in degrees.

* **Angle** 32; **Equation** 79; **Formula** 75; **Function** 92; **Inverse function** 92; **Rearranging an equation** 79; **Right-angled triangle** 37; **Side** 34; **Squaring** 8 (**Square number**); **Sum** 14 (**Addition**); **Triangle** 37.

Cosine ratio (cos)

The formula*:

$$\text{cosine } \theta = \frac{\text{length of adjacent side}}{\text{length of hypotenuse}}$$

Use the cosine ratio if you know or need to know the **adjacent side** or the **hypotenuse**.

For example, to find side b of this triangle, substitute the known values into the cosine ratio:

$$\cos \theta = \frac{\text{length of adjacent side}}{\text{length of hypotenuse}}$$

$$\cos 36° = \frac{10}{b}$$

Rearrange* the formula to solve for b:

$$b = \frac{10}{\cos 36°}$$

Use the "cos" button on your calculator to find the value of cos 36°, and so solve the equation*:

$$b = \frac{10}{0.809\,016\,99}$$

$$b = 12.36\text{cm (2 d.p.)}$$

Side b is 12.36cm long (to 2 d.p.).

Tangent ratio (tan)

The formula*:

$$\text{tangent } \theta = \frac{\text{length of opposite side}}{\text{length of adjacent side}}$$

Use the tangent ratio if you know or need to know the **opposite** or **adjacent side**.

For example, to find the length of side c in this triangle, substitute the known values into the tangent ratio:

$$\tan \theta = \frac{\text{length of opposite side}}{\text{length of adjacent side}}$$

$$\tan 50° = \frac{c}{5}$$

Rearrange* the formula to solve for c:

$$c = 5 \times \tan 50°$$

Use the "tan" button on your calculator to find the value of tan 50°, and so solve the equation*:

$$c = 1.191\,753\,59 \times 5$$

$$c = 5.96\text{cm (2 d.p.)}$$

Side c is 5.96cm long (to 2 d.p.).

SOH CAH TOA

A made-up word useful for remembering the sine, cosine and tangent ratios. It is pronounced *"sock-a-toe-a"* and it stands for:

$$\text{Sin} = \frac{\text{Opposite}}{\text{Hypotenuse}} \quad \text{(SOH)}$$

$$\text{Cos} = \frac{\text{Adjacent}}{\text{Hypotenuse}} \quad \text{(CAH)}$$

$$\text{Tan} = \frac{\text{Opposite}}{\text{Adjacent}} \quad \text{(TOA)}$$

Another way to remember trigonometry ratios is by the saying **"Some Old Horses / Can Always Hear / Their Owners Approach."**

Finding unknown angles

The **sine**, **cosine** and **tangent ratios** can also be used to find the value of an unknown angle in a right-angled triangle*.

The **sin⁻¹** button on your calculator gives the angle that has a sine of $x°$. This is the inverse* of the sine, and is sometimes called **arcsin**.

The **cos⁻¹** button on your calculator gives the angle that has a cosine of $x°$. This is the inverse of the cosine, and is sometimes called **arccos**.

The **tan⁻¹** button on your calculator gives the angle that has a tangent of $x°$. This is the inverse of the tangent and is sometimes called **arctan**.

For example, the lengths of the **hypotenuse** and **adjacent side** of this triangle are known. So, to find angle θ, use the **cosine ratio**:

$$\cos \theta = \frac{\text{length of adjacent side}}{\text{length of hypotenuse}}$$

$$\cos \theta = \frac{6}{12}$$

$$\cos \theta = \frac{1}{2} = 0.5$$

Rearrange* the formula* to solve for θ:

$$\theta = \cos^{-1} 0.5$$

Use the inverse cos button (cos⁻¹ or arccos) on your calculator to find the value of θ:

$$\cos^{-1} 0.5 = 60°$$

Angle θ is 60°.

Non-right-angled triangles

If a triangle does not contain a right angle*, then the sine*, cosine* and tangent* ratios cannot be used directly to calculate the sizes of sides* and angles*. Instead, other relationships, such as the **sine** and **cosine rule**, must be used.

The sine rule

The formula*:

$$\frac{a}{\sin A} = \frac{b}{\sin B} = \frac{c}{\sin C}$$

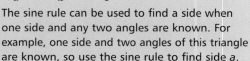

This can be rearranged as:

$$\frac{\sin A}{a} = \frac{\sin B}{b} = \frac{\sin C}{c}$$

The sine rule can be used to find a side when one side and any two angles are known. For example, one side and two angles of this triangle are known, so use the sine rule to find side a.

$$\frac{a}{\sin A} = \frac{b}{\sin B}$$

$$\frac{a}{\sin 40°} = \frac{12}{\sin 95°}$$

$$\frac{a}{0.642\,787\,60} = \frac{12}{0.996\,194\,69}$$

$$a = \frac{12}{0.996\,194\,69} \times 0.642\,787\,60$$

$a = 12.045\,838\,15 \times 0.642\,787\,60$

The equation has been rearranged* to solve for a.*

$a = 7.74$cm (3 s.f.)

Side a is 7.74cm (to 3 s.f.).

The sine rule can also be used to find an angle when two sides and an opposite angle are known. In this case, use the rearranged sine rule, as the unknown angle is the numerator* and so it is more convenient to solve for A.

$$\frac{\sin A}{a} = \frac{\sin B}{b}$$

$$\frac{\sin A}{10} = \frac{\sin 35°}{8}$$

$$\sin A = \frac{\sin 35°}{8} \times 10$$

$\sin A = 0.071\,697\,05 \times 10$

$\sin A = 0.716\,970\,5$

$A = \sin^{-1} 0.716\,970\,5$

The equation has been rearranged* to solve for A.*

$A = 45.8°$ (3 s.f.)

Angle A is 45.8° (to 3 s.f.).

The cosine rule

The formula*:

$$a^2 = b^2 + c^2 - 2bc \cos A$$

and its relations:

$$b^2 = a^2 + c^2 - 2ac \cos A$$

and

$$c^2 = a^2 + b^2 - 2ab \cos A$$

These can also be rearranged to give:

$$\cos A = \frac{b^2 + c^2 - a^2}{2bc}$$

$$\cos B = \frac{a^2 + c^2 - b^2}{2ac}$$

and

$$\cos C = \frac{a^2 + b^2 - c^2}{2ab}$$

The cosine rule can be used to find the length of the third side when the length of two sides and the included angle* are known. For example, in this triangle, two sides and the included angle are known, so use the cosine rule to find the length of side a.

$$a^2 = b^2 + c^2 - 2bc \cos A$$

$$a^2 = 10^2 + 15^2 - (2 \times 10 \times 15 \times \cos 50°)$$

$$a^2 = 100 + 225 - (300 \times 0.642\,787\,61)$$

$$a^2 = 325 - 192.836\,283$$

$$a^2 = 132.163\,717$$

$a = 11.5$ (3 s.f.)

Side a is 11.5cm (to 3 s.f.).

The cosine rule can also be used to find an angle when the lengths of all three sides are known. For example, three sides of this triangle are known. In this case, rearrange the rule to solve for the unknown angle.

$$\cos A = \frac{b^2 + c^2 - a^2}{2bc}$$

$$\cos A = \frac{6^2 + 5^2 - 7^2}{2 \times 6 \times 5}$$

$$\cos A = \frac{12}{60}$$

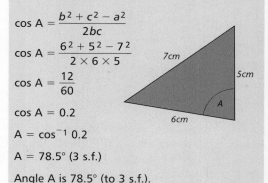

$\cos A = 0.2$

$A = \cos^{-1} 0.2$

$A = 78.5°$ (3 s.f.)

Angle A is 78.5° (to 3 s.f.).

* **Angle** 32; **Area** 55; **Cosine ratio** 61; **Equation** 79; **Formula** 75; **Included angle** 37 (**Angles in a triangle**); **Numerator** 17; **Rearranging an equation** 79; **Right angle** 32; **Sides** 34; **Sine graph** 64; **Sine ratio** 60; **Tangent ratio** 61.

The ambiguous case

If you know the lengths of two sides of a triangle and an angle that is not the included angle*, the triangle can have two possible solutions. This is called the **ambiguous case**, as you do not have enough information about the triangle to draw it. (You can find out how to construct a triangle with two solutions on page 49.)

For example, a triangle with side a 12cm, side b 10cm and angle B 50°, could look like either of these:

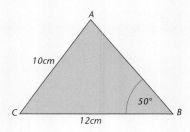

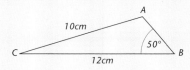

Angle A is quite different in each of these triangles. Using the sine rule to find angle A:

$$\frac{\sin A}{12} = \frac{\sin 50°}{10}$$

$$\sin A = \frac{\sin 50°}{10} \times 12$$

$$\sin A = 0.919\,253\,33$$

$$A = \sin^{-1} 0.919\,253\,33$$

$$= 66.8° \text{ (to 3 s.f.)}$$

This angle is correct for the first triangle. To find the second value of angle A, subtract the first value from 180°:

$$180° - 66.8° = 113.2°$$

So the possible values of angle A are 66.8° and 113.2°. You can check that this is correct using the sine graph*. If only one solution is needed, always give the smallest answer. (Calculators give this answer automatically.)

Area of a triangle

When working with trigonometry, the area* of a triangle can be calculated using the formula*:

$$\textbf{area} = \tfrac{1}{2}ab \sin C$$

where C is the angle you have been given and is the included angle* between sides a and b.

For example, in this triangle, two sides and the included angle are known, so the area can be calculated as:

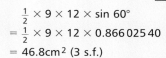

$$\tfrac{1}{2} \times 9 \times 12 \times \sin 60°$$

$$= \tfrac{1}{2} \times 9 \times 12 \times 0.866\,025\,40$$

$$= 46.8\text{cm}^2 \text{ (3 s.f.)}$$

If you do not know the length of two sides and their included angle, you will need to calculate these using the **sine** and **cosine rules** before you can calculate the area of the triangle.

For example, the sides of the triangle below are 6cm, 12cm and 15cm.

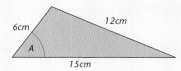

To find the area, first find the value of A. As all sides are known, use the rearranged cosine rule:

$$\cos A = \frac{15^2 + 6^2 - 12^2}{(2 \times 15 \times 6)}$$

$$\cos A = \frac{117}{180}$$

$$\cos A = 0.65$$

$$A = \cos^{-1} 0.65$$

$$= 49.458\,398\,13 = 49.5° \text{ (3 s.f.)}$$

Then calculate the area of the triangle:

$$\tfrac{1}{2} \times 12 \times 15 \times \sin 49.458\,398\,13$$

(Use the unrounded value of A here as the final answer will be rounded.)

$$= \tfrac{1}{2} \times 12 \times 15 \times 0.759\,934\,21$$

$$= 68.4\text{cm}^2 \text{ (3 s.f.)}$$

So, the area of the triangle is 68.4cm² (3 s.f.).

Trigonometric or circular graphs

Sine graph or sine curve

A graph* of sine* θ plotted for every value of θ. It gives a curve called a **sine wave**. The pattern of the curve repeats every 360°, so it is described as having a **period** of 360°. The graph can be used to find the value of sin x, where x is any angle*.

For example, where x = 90°, y = 1, so the value of sin 90° is 1.

Graph of the function* y = sin x

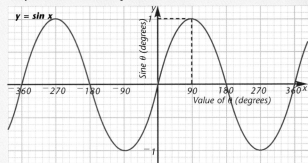

Cosine graph or cosine curve

A graph* of cosine* θ plotted for every value of θ. The pattern of the curve repeats every 360°, so it is described as having a **period** of 360°. The cosine graph is similar to the **sine wave**, but is in a different position along the x-axis. This graph can be used to find the value of cos x, where x is any angle*.

For example, where x = 180°, y = ⁻1, so the value of cos 180° is ⁻1.

Graph of the function* y = cos x

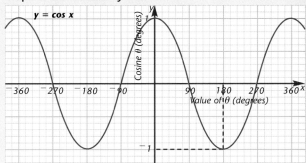

Tangent graph or tangent curve

A graph* of tangent* θ plotted for every value of θ. It is a non-continuous (broken) graph which repeats every 180°, so it is described as having a **period** of 180°. The graph breaks at the point where tan θ is an infinite number. (Tan 90° will give an error on your calculator.) These breaks are sometimes called **discontinuities**. This graph can be used to find the value of tan x, where x is any angle*. For example, where x = 45°, y = 1, so the value of tan 45° is 1.

Graph of the function* y = tan x

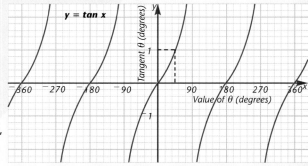

Variations on graphs

Variations of the **sine** and **cosine** graphs are produced when their functions* are changed slightly. The graph y = sin x can be changed to y = a sin x, and y = cos x can be changed to y = a cos x (where a does not equal zero). These variations affect the height, called the **amplitude**, of the graphs.

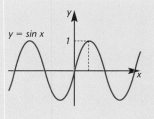

The graph y = sin x has a maximum value of 1.

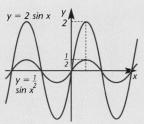

The graph y = 2 sin x has a maximum value of 2. The graph y = ½ sin x has a maximum value of ½ and so on.

* **Angle** 32; **Area** 55; **Compasses** 47; **Cones** 68; **Cosine** 60; **Cylinders** 67; **Function** 92;
Graph (Algebraic) 80; **Sine** 60; **Spheres** 69; **Tangent** 60.

CIRCLES

A **circle** is a flat closed curve, every point on the edge of which is the same distance from a given point, called the **center** of the circle. A circle can be drawn using a pair of compasses*. Circles have certain characteristics that help us to calculate their properties such as **circumference** and area*, as well as the volume of cylinders*, cones* and spheres*.

Center

All points on the edge of this circle are the same distance from the center.

Parts of a circle

Circumference
The total distance around the edge of a circle.

Circumference

Arc
Part of the **circumference** of a circle. If a circle's circumference is divided into two arcs of unequal length, the longer arc is called the **major arc** and the shorter one is the **minor arc**.

Minor arc

Major arc

Semicircular arc
An **arc** that is half the **circumference** of a circle.

Semicircular arc

Semicircular arc

Quadrant arc
An **arc** that is one quarter of the **circumference** of a circle.

Quadrant arc

Radius (plural is **radii**)
Any straight line drawn from the **center** of a circle to a point on its **circumference**. The radius is half the **diameter**.

Radius

Diameter
A straight line through the **center** of a circle, joining two points on the **circumference**. The diameter is twice the **radius**.

Diameter

Sector
Part of a circle formed by an **arc** and two **radii**. The smaller part of the circle is called the **minor sector**, and the larger part is called the **major sector**.

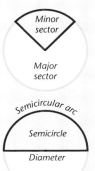

Minor sector

Major sector

Semicircle
Half a circle, formed by the **diameter** and a **semicircular arc**.

Semicircular arc

Semicircle

Diameter

Quadrant
Quarter of a circle, formed by two **radii** that are at right angles (90°) to each other, and a **quadrant arc**.

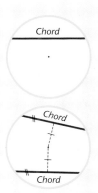

Quadrant arc

Quadrant

Radius

Radius

Chord
A straight line joining any two points on a circle. Any two chords of the same length that are drawn within a circle are **equidistant**, or the same distance, from the **center** of the circle. This also means that if two chords are equidistant from the center of a circle, they will always be the same length.

Chord

Chord

Chord

Segment
Part of a circle formed either side of a **chord**. The larger part is called the **major segment**. The smaller one is called the **minor segment**.

Minor segment

Major segment

Internet links For links to useful websites on **circles**, go to *www.usborne-quicklinks.com*

CALCULATIONS INVOLVING CIRCLES

Pi (π)

Pi is the ratio* of the circumference* of any circle to its diameter*, or in other words, the distance around the edge of a circle compared with the distance across it. Pi is an irrational number* that has been calculated to more than a trillion decimal places, but its value is approximately 3.142 (3 d.p.) or $\frac{22}{7}$. It is symbolized by the Greek letter π. Pi is used when measuring the area and volume of circles, **cylinders**, cones* and spheres*.

 Use the Pi key on your scientific calculator to display the value of Pi.

Calculators give the value of Pi to several decimal places, e.g. 3.141 592 654, which is accurate enough for most calculations. (The number of decimal places varies from one calculator to another.)

To find the circumference of a circle

Multiply the diameter* by **Pi** (π). The formula* for finding the circumference* is:

circumference = πd or 2πr

where r is the radius* and d is the diameter of the circle.

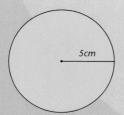

The circumference of this circle is:
$$2 \times \pi \times 5$$
$$= 2 \times 3.142 \times 5$$
$$= 31.42cm$$

If the circumference of a circle is known, you can calculate the length of the radius or diameter using the following formula:

$$r = \frac{circumference}{2\pi}$$

For example, if the circumference of this circle is 26cm, its radius is:

$$\frac{26}{2 \times \pi}$$
$$= \frac{26}{6.283...}$$
$$= 4.14cm \text{ (3 s.f.)}$$

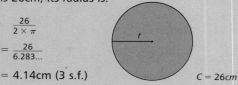

C = 26cm

To find the length of an arc

Draw a straight line from each end of the arc* to the center of the circle and measure the angle* that is created. The length of the arc is the same fraction of the total circumference* as the angle at the center of the circle is of 360° (the total number of degrees in a full revolution):

$$\frac{l}{C} = \frac{x}{360}$$

where l is the length of the arc, C is the circumference and x is the angle at the center of the circle. This means that:

$$l = \frac{x}{360} \times C$$

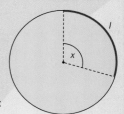

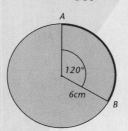

For example, to find the length of the arc AB:
$$\frac{x}{360} \times C$$
$$= \frac{120}{360} \times 2\pi r$$
$$= \frac{1}{3} \times 2 \times \pi \times 6$$
$$= 12.6cm \text{ (3 s.f.)}$$

Area of a circle

A circle has a radius* (r) and a circumference* (2πr). If you sliced up the circle and arranged the sectors* as shown below, the resulting shape would be roughly rectangular, with an area of πr × r, or πr².

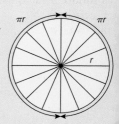

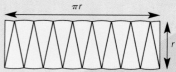

It therefore follows that the area* of the original circle can be found using the same formula:

area = πr²

For example, the area of this circle is:
$$\pi \times 4^2$$
$$= \pi \times 16$$
$$= 50.3cm^2 \text{ (3 s.f.)}$$

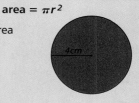

4cm

* **Angle** 32; **Arc** 65; **Area** 55; **Circumference** 65; **Cone** 68; **Diameter** 65; **Formula** 75; **Irrational number** 9; **Net, Prism** 41; **Radius** 65; **Ratio** 24; **Rectangle** 39; **Sector** 65; **Sphere** 69; **Surface area** 57; **Volume** 58.

To find the area of a sector

The area* of a sector* is the same fraction of the total area of the circle as the angle at the center of the circle is of 360° (the total number of degrees in a full revolution).

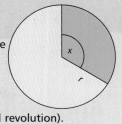

$$\text{area of a sector} = \frac{x}{360} \times \pi r^2$$

where x is the angle at the center.

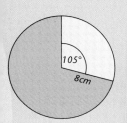

For example, the area of this sector is:

$$\frac{105}{360} \times \pi r^2$$

$$= \frac{105}{360} \times \pi \times 8^2$$

$$= \frac{105}{360} \times \pi \times 64$$

$$= 58.6\text{cm}^2 \text{ (3 s.f.)}$$

Cylinders

A **cylinder** is a prism* with circular bases. A net* of a cylinder shows that its surface area* is made up of a rectangle* and two circles.

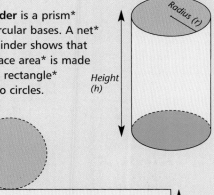

Height (h)

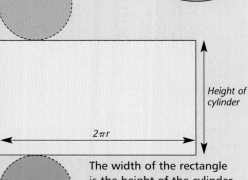

Height of cylinder

$2\pi r$

The width of the rectangle is the height of the cylinder, and the length of the rectangle is equal to the circle's circumference*.

To find the curved surface area of a cylinder

The length of the rectangle is the same length as the circumference* of the circles, so to find the curved surface area*, use:

$$\text{area} = 2\pi r \times h \quad \text{or} \quad 2\pi rh$$

where π is approximately 3.142. For example, the curved surface area of this cylinder is:

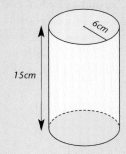

6cm

15cm

$$2 \times \pi \times 6 \times 15$$

$$= 565\text{cm}^2 \text{ (3 s.f.)}$$

To find the total surface area of a cylinder

Add together the area* of the rectangle (the area of the curved surface of the cylinder) and both circles. (Use the formula* **area = πr^2** to find the area of the circles.)

For example, the total surface area* of this cylinder can be calculated as follows:

6cm

15cm

curved surface area
$$2 \times \pi \times 6 \times 15$$
$$= 565.486\text{cm}^2$$

area of both circles
$$2 \times \pi \times 6^2$$
$$= 226.194\text{cm}^2$$

surface area of cylinder
$$565.486 + 226.194$$
$$= 791.68$$
$$= 792\text{cm}^2 \text{ (3 s.f.)}$$

To find the volume of a cylinder

Multiply the area* of the cylinder's base by the height of the cylinder:

$$\text{volume} = \pi r^2 \times h \quad \text{or} \quad \pi r^2 h$$

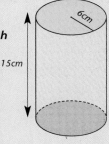

6cm

15cm

For example, the volume* of this cylinder is:

$$\pi \times 6^2 \times 15$$
$$= \pi \times 36 \times 15$$
$$= 1696\text{cm}^3 \text{ (4 s.f.)}$$

Cones

A **cone** is a pyramid* with a circular base. If you were to cut down the pink line of the cone on the right, and open out the shape, you would find that its curved surface area* is a sector* of a circle.

The base of a cone is a circle with a radius of r.*

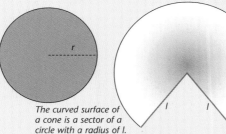

The curved surface of a cone is a sector of a circle with a radius of l.

To find the curved surface area of a cone

The length of the curved edge of the sector* is $2\pi r$, because it is equal to the circumference* of the smaller circle. The radius* of the large circle (of which the sector is a part) is the same as the slant height* of the cone (l), so the circumference of the large circle is $2\pi l$.

The length of the curved edge of the sector compared with the circumference of the larger circle is $\frac{2\pi r}{2\pi l}$ which cancels down to $\frac{r}{l}$. The area* of the sector compared with the area of the circle of which it is a part is also therefore $\frac{r}{l}$.

The area of the sector is calculated by:

$$\frac{r}{l} \times \pi l^2 = \frac{r \times \pi l^2}{l} = r\pi l \text{ or } \pi r l$$

which is in effect multiplying Pi* by the radius of the circular base and then by the slant height. Therefore, to find the curved surface area of a cone, use:

curved surface area = $\pi r l$

For example, the curved surface area of this cone is:

$\pi \times 4 \times 10$
$= \pi \times 40$
$= 126\text{cm}^2$ (3 s.f.)

10cm
4cm

To find the total surface area of a cone

Add the area* of the base to the curved surface area. For the area of the circle, use **area = πr^2** and for the curved surface area use **surface area = $\pi r l$**, where r is the radius* of the base and l is the slant height*.

For example, the total curved surface area of this cone can be calculated as follows:

curved surface area
$\pi \times 4 \times 10$
$= 125.66\text{cm}^2$

area of circle
$\pi \times 16$
$= 50.26\text{cm}^2$

total surface area of cone
$125.66 + 50.26$
$= 176\text{cm}^2$ (3 s.f.)

10cr
4cm

To find the volume of a cone

The volume* of any pyramid* is a third of the volume of a prism* with the same base and height. Therefore, the volume of a cone is one third of the volume of a cylinder with the same size base and perpendicular height*. To find the volume* of a cone, use:

volume = $\frac{1}{3}\pi r^2 h$

where h is the perpendicular height.

For example, the volume of this cone is:

$\frac{1}{3} \times \pi \times 4^2 \times 8$
$= \frac{1}{3} \times \pi \times 16 \times 8$
$= 134\text{cm}^3$ (3 s.f.)

8cm
4cm

If the radius* and the slant height* are given, the perpendicular height can be calculated using the Pythagorean theorem*. For example, to find the perpendicular height of a cone with a radius of 3cm and a slant height of 7cm, use:

$a^2 + b^2 = c^2$
$a^2 + 3^2 = 7^2$
$a^2 + 9 = 49$
$a^2 = 40$
$a = 6.32455532$

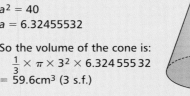

So the volume of the cone is:

$\frac{1}{3} \times \pi \times 3^2 \times 6.324\,555\,32$
$= 59.6\text{cm}^3$ (3 s.f.)

7cm
3cm

* **Area** 55; **Chord** 65; **Circumference** 65; **Cross section** 41; **Diameter** 65; **Line of symmetry** 42; **Line segment** 30; **Perpendicular height** 56 (Area of a triangle); **Pi** 66; **Prism** 41; **Pyramid** 41; **Pythagorean theorem** 38; **Radius**, **Sector** 65; **Slant height** 41; **Surface area** 57; **Symmetry** 42; **Volume** 58.

Spheres

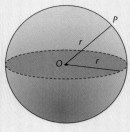

A **sphere** is a perfectly round solid. Every point on the surface of a sphere is an equal distance from the fixed point at its center.

Any point (P) on a sphere is an equal distance from the center (O). This distance is the radius* (r) of the sphere.

To find the surface area of a sphere

Multiply the area* of a circle of radius* r by 4.

$$\text{surface area} = 4\pi r^2$$

where r is the radius.

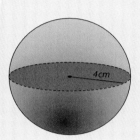

For example, the surface area* of this sphere is:

$4 \times \pi \times 4^2$

$= 4 \times \pi \times 16$

$= 201 \text{cm}^2$ (3 s.f.)

To find the volume of a sphere

Use the formula:

$$\text{volume} = \frac{4}{3}\pi r^3$$

where r is the radius of the cross section* of the sphere.

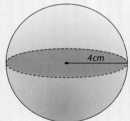

For example, the volume* of this sphere is:

$\frac{4}{3} \times \pi \times 4^3$

$= \frac{4}{3} \times \pi \times 64$

$= 268 \text{cm}^2$ (3 s.f.)

Hemisphere

Half a **sphere**. The volume* of a hemisphere is half the volume of a sphere with the same radius*. The surface area* of a hemisphere is half the surface area of a sphere of the same radius, plus the area* of the circle that forms the flat surface.

A hemisphere is half a sphere.

Ellipses

An **ellipse** is a closed symmetrical* curve, like a squashed or stretched circle. Any chord* that passes through the center of the ellipse is a diameter*. There are two diameters in an ellipse that are also lines of symmetry*. The longer diameter is called the **major axis**, and the shorter one is the **minor axis**.

An ellipse has two lines of symmetry, the major axis and the minor axis.

The line segment* from the center of the ellipse to the edge along the major axis is called the **semi-major axis**. The line segment from the center of the ellipse to the edge along the minor axis is called the **semi-minor axis**. These are used to calculate the area* of an ellipse.

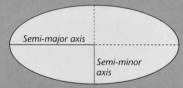

The semi-major and semi-minor axes of an ellipse are needed to find its area.

To calculate the area of an ellipse, use:

$$\text{area} = \pi a b$$

where a is the length of the semi-major axis and b is the length of the semi-minor axis.

For example, the area of this ellipse is:

$\pi \times 4.5 \times 3$

$= 42.4 \text{cm}^2$ (3 s.f.)

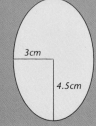

Internet links For links to useful websites on **circles**, go to *www.usborne-quicklinks.com*

ANGLES IN A CIRCLE

A circle has no corners, so it has no angles*. However, the various parts of a circle form angles that all have certain properties.

Naming angles

An angle can be named with reference to the points at the ends of its arms*. For example, in this triangle, the angle at vertex* A is referred to as ∠BAC or ∠CAB, the angle at B as ∠ABC or ∠CBA and the angle at C as ∠ACB or ∠BCA. These can also be written as BÂC, AB̂C and AĈB, respectively.

Subtended angle

An angle formed by lines drawn from both ends of a chord* or arc* to the center of the circle, or a point on the circumference*. The angle is said to be **subtended at** the center or circumference and it is said to be **subtended by** the chord or arc.

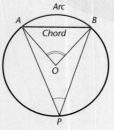

∠APB is subtended at the circumference by the chord AB and the arc AB.

The perpendicular bisector of a chord

A line at right angles* to, and crossing through the midpoint* of, a chord*. The perpendicular bisector of a chord always passes through the center of a circle (O).

Any radius* that passes through the midpoint of a chord (AB) is perpendicular (at 90°) to that chord. If points O and A are joined and points O and B are joined, the perpendicular bisector creates two congruent* right-angled triangles*.

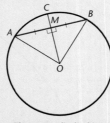

The perpendicular bisector OC crosses chord AB at its midpoint M. Angles ∠OMA and ∠OMB are both right angles.

Properties of angles

The properties described below are shared by all **subtended angles**.

Angles at the center

The angle **subtended** by an arc* or chord* at the center of a circle is always twice the angle subtended at the circumference* by the same arc.

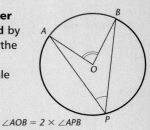

∠AOB = 2 × ∠APB

Angles at the circumference

Angles **subtended** at the circumference* by equal arcs* or chords* are equal.

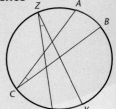

Where arc XY = arc AB, ∠XZY = ∠ACB.

Angles subtended by the same arc or chord

Angles **subtended** by the same arc* or chord* are equal, provided that they are in the same segment*.

This diagram shows how angles ∠APB, ∠AQB and ∠ARB are all subtended by the same arc and are in the major segment of the circle.

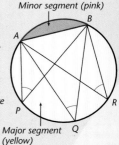

Minor segment (pink)

Major segment (yellow)

∠APB = ∠AQB = ∠ARB

Angles in a semicircle

Any angle **subtended** at the center of a circle by a semicircular arc* is 180°.

It follows, then, that any angle subtended by the same arc at the circumference* is 90°, as this is always half of the angle at the center (see *Angles at the center*, above). This applies to any angle subtended by a diameter*: it is always a right angle*.

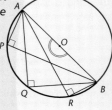

∠AOB = 180°
∠APB = ∠AQB = ∠ARB = 90°

* **Angle** 32; **Arc** 65; **Arms** 32; **Chord** 65; **Circumference** 65; **Congruent triangles** 38; **Diameter** 65; **Exterior angle**, **Interior angle** 34; **Midpoint** 48; **Perpendicular** 30; **Quadrilateral** 39; **Radius** 65; **Right angle** 32; **Right-angled triangle** 37; **Segment, Semicircular arc** 65; **Vertex** 34 **(Polygons)**; **Whole turn** 32.

Tangents

A straight line that touches a curve at a **point of contact** is called a **tangent**. When a tangent touches a circle, it is called a **tangent to the circle** and has certain properties.

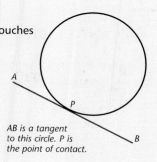

AB is a tangent to this circle. P is the point of contact.

First property

A **tangent** to a circle is always perpendicular* to a radius* drawn at the **point of contact**.

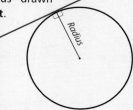

Right angles* are formed at the point where the tangent AB meets the radius of the circle.

Second property

Two **tangents** to a circle drawn from the same point are equal in length.

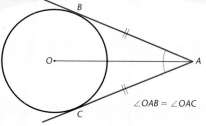

The length of tangent AB is equal to the length of tangent AC.

∠OAB = ∠OAC

The diagram above also shows that the line OA bisects ∠BAC, so ∠OAB and ∠OAC are equal.

Alternate segment property

The angle formed between a **tangent** and a chord* drawn from its **point of contact** is equal to any angle **subtended** by the chord in the alternate segment. The **alternate segment** is the segment on the opposite side of the chord to the angle formed between the tangent and the chord at the point of contact.

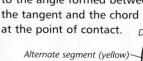

Alternate segment (yellow)

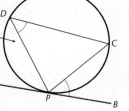

Angle ∠BPC is formed between the tangent AB and the chord PC at the point of contact (P). Angle ∠PDC is in the alternate segment, so ∠BPC = ∠PDC.

Cyclic quadrilaterals

A quadrilateral* that has each of its vertices* on the circumference* of a circle is called a **cyclic quadrilateral**. Angles within a cyclic quadrilateral have some important properties.

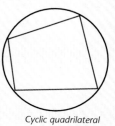

Cyclic quadrilateral

First property of cyclic quadrilaterals

Opposite angles in a cyclic quadrilateral are supplementary, which means that they add up to 180°.

An angle **subtended** at the center of a circle is always twice the angle subtended at the circumference* by the same arc* (see *Angles at the center*, page 70). This means that the angles at the center of the diagram below can be labeled as 2a and 2b.

Angles 2a and 2b add up to 360°, because together they make a whole turn*, so angles a and b, which are half of that, must add up to 180°.

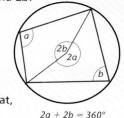

$2a + 2b = 360°$
$\therefore a + b = 180°$

Second property of cyclic quadrilaterals

The exterior angle* is equal to the opposite interior angle*.

The diagram below shows that:

Angle x is equal to 180° − a, because angles on a line add up to 180°.

Angle y is equal to 180° − a, because opposite angles in a cyclic quadrilateral are supplementary.

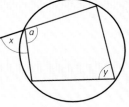

Therefore angles x and y are equal.

$x = 180° - a$
$y = 180° - a$
$\therefore x = y$

MEASUREMENT

In everyday life, we need to measure sizes, quantities and amounts of things, and be able to share that information accurately with other people. Using standard units of measurement is a way of making sure that everyone interprets measurements in the same way. Two widely accepted measurement systems are the **US customary units** and **metric** system.

US customary units

A system of measurement that originally developed in the UK and is used in various forms in many English-speaking countries, including the USA. In some countries, these units have been partly replaced by the metric system.

Metric system

A decimal system* of measurement, used in many countries worldwide. The metric system is based on tens, hundreds and thousands, making calculations more straightforward.

Length

The distance between two fixed points.

Mass

The amount of matter that an object contains. Mass is different from **weight**, which is the measure of the pull of gravity on an object's mass. Weight can change so, for example, a person weighs far less on the Moon (where gravity is very weak) than on Earth, but their mass stays the same.

Capacity

The internal volume of an object or container.

US customary units

Units of length	Abbreviation	Equal to
Inch	"	
Foot	'	12 inches
Yard	yd	3 feet
Mile		1760 yards

Units of capacity	Abbreviation	Equal to
Fluid ounce	fl. oz	
Cup		8 ounces
Pint	pt	16 fluid ounces
Quart	qt	2 pints
Gallon	gal	8 pints

Units of mass	Abbreviation	Equal to
Ounce	oz	
Pound	lb	16 ounces

Metric units

Units of length	Abbreviation	Equal to
Millimeter	mm	
Centimeter	cm	10 millimeters
Meter	m	100 centimeters
Kilometer	km	1000 meters

Units of mass	Abbreviation	Equal to
Milligram	mg	
Gram	g	1000 milligrams
Kilogram	kg	1000 grams
Tonne	t	1000 kilograms

Units of capacity	Abbreviation	Equal to
Milliliter	ml	
Centiliter	cl	100 milliliters
Liter	l	1000 milliliters

US customary unit	Metric equivalent
1 foot	≈ 30 centimeters
5 miles	≈ 8 kilometers
2.2 pounds	≈ 1 kilogram
2.12 pints	≈ 1 liter
1 gallon	≈ 3.79 liters

(≈ means "approximately equal to")

*Bearing 53 (**Three-figure bearings**); **Decimal system** 19; **Formula** 75; **Graph** (**Line**) 110; **Horizontal** 30; **Vector** 45; **Volume** 58.

Measures of motion

Speed

A measure of distance moved over time. The rate of speed is most commonly measured in miles per hour (mph), kilometers per hour (kph, km/h or kmh⁻¹) or meters per second (m/s or ms⁻¹). The formula* for measuring the rate of speed is:

$$\text{rate} = \frac{\text{distance}}{\text{time}}$$

For example, if a car travels at a steady rate, covering 180 miles in 3 hours, its rate is 60mph $(\frac{180}{3})$.

If a car travels 70 miles in the first hour then 55 miles in each of the next two hours, it will still cover 180 miles in the same time as if it had traveled steadily at 60mph. The steady rate that enables the same distance to be covered in the same amount of time is called the **average rate**.

The formula for measuring average rate is:

$$\text{average rate} = \frac{\text{total distance}}{\text{total time}}$$

The formula for rate can be rearranged to give formulas for measuring distance and time:

$$\text{distance} = \text{rate} \times \text{time}$$

$$\text{time} = \frac{\text{distance}}{\text{rate}}$$

You can use the grid below to remind you of these formulas. In this grid, D stands for distance, R for rate and T for time.

To find the formula for distance, cover up the D and you are left with the formula R × T.

Cover up the R to discover the formula for rate $\frac{D}{T}$.

To find the formula for time, cover up the T and you are left with $\frac{D}{R}$.

Compound measure

A measurement involving more than one unit. For example, **speed** is a compound measure involving distance and time. Another common compound measure is **density**, which involves **mass** and volume*. (For more on density, see page 59.)

Distance-time graph

A graph* showing **speed**, drawn by plotting units of distance against units of time.

A straight diagonal line on a distance-time graph represents an object moving at a constant speed.

This graph shows an object moving at a constant rate of 5mph (total distance divided by total time).

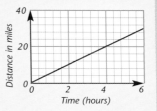

A horizontal line on a distance-time graph represents an object at rest.*

This graph shows an object that has no speed, so is not moving.

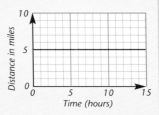

Velocity

A measure of distance moved in a particular direction over a period of time. Velocity is a vector* quantity. Like **speed**, it is most commonly measured in miles per hour (mph), kilometers per hour (kph, km/h or kmh⁻¹) or meters per second (m/s or ms⁻¹). Unlike speed, a direction must also be given. For example the velocity of a light aircraft might be 110kph on a bearing* of 050°.

Acceleration

The rate of change of **velocity**. Acceleration is a vector* quantity. It is usually measured in meters per second per second, which is shortened to m/s² or ms⁻². To calculate acceleration, use:

$$\text{acceleration} = \frac{\text{change of velocity}}{\text{time taken}}$$

For example, if a train changes speed from 6m/s to 12m/s in 3s, its acceleration is:

$$\frac{12 - 6}{3} = \frac{6}{3} = 2\text{m/s}^2$$

The acceleration of the train is 2m/s² in the direction of the track.

Deceleration

Negative **acceleration**, that is, the object is slowing down.

TIME

A **day** is the time it takes the Earth to spin around once. This period is divided into 24 **hours**, which can be broken down into smaller units: **minutes** and **seconds**. These are the units used in telling the time.

Digital clocks and watches often use the 24-hour clock. This picture shows what the time 4:20pm would look like on a digital display.

Minute (min)

There are 60 minutes in an **hour**.

Second (s or sec)

There are 60 seconds in a **minute**. A second is the smallest unit on a standard clock. It is approximately the time taken by one heartbeat or to say the word "hippopotamus."

Millisecond (ms or msec)

There are 1,000 milliseconds in a **second**. Milliseconds are used to measure very fast speeds*, such as the rate at which a computer processes information.

12-hour clock

A time system in which the hours in a day are divided into two groups of 12.

Hours in the first group, between **midnight** (12 o'clock at night) and **noon** (12 o'clock in the middle of the day) are described as "am." This stands for the Latin words *ante meridiem*, meaning "before noon." Hours in the second group, between noon and midnight, are described as "pm." This stands for the Latin words *post meridiem*, meaning "after noon."

The **minutes** are written after a colon. For example, 15 minutes past 6 in the morning is written as 6:15am.

24-hour clock

A time system in which the 24 hours of the day are not expressed as am or pm, but are numbered straight through from 0 to 23. The numbers 0 to 9 are written with a 0 in front of them, e.g. 01, 02... Times written using the 24-hour clock are expressed as four figures, and the **minutes** are not separated from the hours by a colon. For example, 20 minutes past 2 in the afternoon is written as 1420. The table below shows how each hour of the day is written in the **12-hour clock** and 24-hour clock.

12 hour clock	24 hour clock
12:00 midnight	0000 hours
1:00am	0100 hours
2:00am	0200 hours
3:00am	0300 hours
4:00am	0400 hours
5:00am	0500 hours
6:00am	0600 hours
7:00am	0700 hours
8:00am	0800 hours
9:00am	0900 hours
10:00am	1000 hours
11:00am	1100 hours
12:00 noon	1200 hours
1:00pm	1300 hours
2:00pm	1400 hours
3:00pm	1500 hours
4:00pm	1600 hours
5:00pm	1700 hours
6:00pm	1800 hours
7:00pm	1900 hours
8:00pm	2000 hours
9:00pm	2100 hours
10:00pm	2200 hours
11:00pm	2300 hours

At 10:20am, it is daytime.

At 10:20pm, it is night.

* **Area of a triangle** 56; **Exponent** 21; **Perpendicular height** 56 (**Area of a triangle**); **Speed** 73.

ALGEBRA

Algebra is a branch of mathematics in which letters and symbols are used to express numbers and the relationships between them. Letters from the beginning of the alphabet are used to represent known values, and letters from the end of the alphabet are used to represent unknown values.

In algebra, lower-case letters and symbols, are used to represent the relationships between unknown quantities.

Algebraic expression

A mathematical statement written in algebraic form. An expression can contain any combination of letters or numbers, and often involves the arithmetic operations addition, subtraction, multiplication and division. e.g. $7x - 4$, $14 + (y - 2)$, $12z$.

Any algebraic expression containing two or more terms is called a **polynomial**, or **multinomial**, **expression**. An algebraic expression containing two terms is called a **binomial expression**, e.g. $2x + y$. An algebraic expression containing three terms is a **trinomial expression**, e.g. $3x + y - xy$.

Algebraic identity

A mathematical statement that two **algebraic expressions** are equal, whatever the value of the **variables**. An identity is often indicated by the symbol $\equiv$, e.g. $x + x \equiv 2x$.

Formula

A general rule that is usually expressed algebraically. For example, the area of a triangle* can be expressed by the formula:

$$\text{area} = \tfrac{1}{2}bh$$

where b represents the base and h represents the perpendicular height*.

Variable

An unknown number or quantity represented by a letter. A variable is most commonly represented by the letter x, although other letters can be used as a reminder of the word they are replacing. For example, $d =$ distance, $t =$ time, and so on. Sometimes a variable has a range of values, for example, if y is equal to $2x$, when y is 1, x is $\tfrac{1}{2}$, when y is 2, x is 1, and so on.

Dependent variable

A **variable** with a value that is calculated from other values. For example, the area of a triangle* depends on the values of the base and perpendicular height*, so the area is a dependent variable. The values of the base and height of a triangle do not depend on anything else, so they are examples of **independent variables**.

Constant

A number with a value that is always the same. For example, in the **expression** $y = 2x + 4$, 4 is a constant.

Coefficient

A **constant** that is placed before a **variable** in an **expression**. For example, in the expression $3x + 4y$, the coefficient of the variable x is 3 and the coefficient of the variable y is 4.

Unknown constant coefficients are usually represented by letters from the beginning of the alphabet: a, b, c. For example, $ax + b = y$.

Term

The parts of an **expression** that are separated by a $+$ or $-$ sign. An algebraic term can be a **variable**, a **coefficient**, a **constant** or a combination of these. For example, the terms in the expression $2 + 3y + 5x - 1$ are 2 (constant), $3y$ (coefficient and variable), $5x$ (coefficient and variable) and 1 (constant).

Terms that contain the same letter or combination of letters and same exponents* are **like terms**. Terms that contain different letters or combinations of letters or different exponents are **unlike terms**. For example, xy, yx and $2xy$ are like terms, but $3y$ and y^3 are unlike terms.

Internet links For links to useful websites on **general algebra**, go to *www.usborne-quicklinks.com*

BASIC ALGEBRA

Many of the general rules of numbers also apply to algebra. Pages 76 to 78 contain some number rules that you particularly need to remember. They also contain useful information about different ways in which you can make algebraic expressions* more manageable.

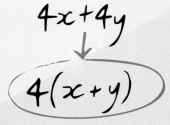

$4x + 4y$

$4(x + y)$

Algebraic expressions can often be rewritten in different ways but still mean the same.

Rules of number and algebra

Parentheses

Parentheses are used to group together algebraic terms*. The term directly in front of the parentheses can be multiplied by each term in the parentheses. For example, $6x - 6y$ can also be written as $6(x - y)$.

Exponents

An exponent* next to a letter indicates that the value is multiplied by itself. The exponent tells you how many times the value should appear in the multiplication, e.g. x^2 means $x \times x$. A negative exponent indicates the reciprocal* of the number with a positive version of the exponent*, e.g. $x^{-2} = \frac{1}{x^2}$.

Powers* of the same letter can be multiplied by adding the exponents or divided by subtracting the second exponent from the first.

$$a^n \times a^m = a^{n+m} \quad \text{and} \quad a^n \div a^m = a^{n-m}$$

Different powers of the same letter cannot be added or subtracted as they are unlike terms*. The other laws of exponents also apply. These are summarized below, but they are explained in greater detail on page 22.

$$a^1 = a$$

$$1^a = 1$$

$$a^0 = 1$$

$$(a^n)^m = a^{n \times m}$$

$$(a \times b)^n = a^n \times b^n$$

$$\left(\frac{a}{b}\right)^m = \frac{a^m}{b^m}$$

$$a^{\frac{m}{n}} = \sqrt[n]{a^m}$$

Multiplication

It is usual to write an algebraic multiplication expression* without a multiplication sign.

e.g. $a \times b \times c$ becomes abc.

The commutative law of multiplication* applies, so $abc = acb = bca = bac = cab = cba$.

e.g. $5 \times 3 \times x = 3 \times 5 \times x = \ldots = 15x$

Directed numbers

Adding a negative term* is the same as subtracting a positive term.

e.g. $2x + (^-x) = 2x - x = x$

Subtracting a negative term is the same as adding a positive term.

e.g. $2x - (^-x) = 2x + x = 3x$

Multiplying or dividing two terms with the same sign ($+$ or $-$) in front will give a positive result.

e.g. $4 \times 3y = 12y$
$^-4 \times ^-3y = 12y$

and $16y \div 4y = 4$
$^-16y \div ^-4y = 4$

Multiplying or dividing two terms with opposite signs will give a negative result.

e.g. $4 \times ^-3y = ^-12y$
and $^-16y \div 4y = ^-4$

PEMDAS (see also page 16)
In an expression* involving mixed arithmetic operations, the operations should be performed in the following order:
Parentheses
Exponents (values raised to a power*)
Multiplication
Division
Addition
Subtraction

Algebraic fractions

Equivalent fractions* can be found by multiplying or dividing the numerator (top value) and the denominator (bottom value) by the same number or letter.

e.g. $\dfrac{3x}{9} = \dfrac{6x}{18} = \dfrac{x}{3} = \dfrac{xy}{3y} = \dfrac{x^2}{3x}$

Algebraic fractions can be added or subtracted by expressing them as fractions with a common denominator. (Algebraic common denominators are like terms*.)

e.g. $\dfrac{3}{2x} + \dfrac{2}{x} = \dfrac{3}{2x} + \dfrac{2 \times 2}{2 \times x} = \dfrac{7}{2x}$

Multiplication expressions involving algebraic fractions can be simplified by multiplying out the numerators and multiplying out the denominators, then canceling* the fraction to its lowest possible terms*.

e.g. $\dfrac{3a}{4} \times \dfrac{a}{3} = \dfrac{\overset{1}{\cancel{3}}a \times a}{4 \times \cancel{3}_1} = \dfrac{a^2}{4}$

Division expressions involving algebraic fractions can be simplified by finding the reciprocal* of the second fraction then multiplying out the numerators, multiplying out the denominators and canceling the fraction, as above.

e.g. $\dfrac{3x}{4} \div \dfrac{x}{2} = \dfrac{3x}{4} \times \dfrac{2}{x}$

$= \dfrac{3x \times 2}{4 \times x} = \dfrac{\overset{1}{3x} \times \overset{1}{\cancel{2}}}{\underset{2}{\cancel{4}} \times \cancel{x}_1} = \dfrac{3}{2} = 1\tfrac{1}{2}$

Substitution

The replacement of the letters in an algebraic expression* with known values is called **substitution**. You might use substitution, for example, when calculating properties of shapes and solids, such as area* or volume*, according to a particular formula*.

For example, the formula for finding the area of a triangle is:

area of triangle $= \tfrac{1}{2}bh$

where b represents the base and h represents the perpendicular height*. To find the area of a triangle with a base of 8cm and height of 7cm, substitute the measurements for the algebraic terms in the formula:

area $= \tfrac{1}{2} \times 8 \times 7 = \tfrac{1}{2} \times 56 = 28\text{cm}^2$

Simplification

Combining the terms* in an algebraic expression* is called **simplifying**.

Expressions involving addition and subtraction can be simplified by adding or subtracting like terms*. For example, to simplify
$3x + 6y + 2y - x$
combine all the x terms:
$\qquad (3x - x) + 6y + 2y$
$\qquad = 2x + 6y + 2y$
then combine all the y terms:
$\qquad 2x + (6y + 2y)$
$\qquad = 2x + 8y$

Expressions involving multiplication can be simplified by multiplying out the terms. For example, to simplify the expression $5a \times 3b$ write the expression out in full:
$\qquad = 5 \times a \times 3 \times b$
then combine the numbers (5×3):
$\qquad = 15 \times a \times b$
then combine the letters $(a \times b)$:
$\qquad = 15ab$

Expressions involving division can be simplified by canceling* out the terms. For example, to simplify $8pq^3 \div 4q$, write the expression as a fraction, then cancel it down:

$$\dfrac{\overset{2}{\cancel{8}} \times p \times \overset{1}{\cancel{q}} \times q \times q}{\cancel{4} \times \cancel{q}_{1}}$$

$$= 2pq^2$$

When simplifying expressions involving fractions, if the numerator and/or denominators contain more than one term, it is often useful to place this part in parentheses. For example, to simplify the expression
$\dfrac{a}{3} + \dfrac{a-1}{2}$

Place numerator in parentheses.	$= \dfrac{a}{3} + \dfrac{(a-1)}{2}$
Find a common denominator.	$= \dfrac{2a}{6} + \dfrac{3(a-1)}{6}$
Multiply out the parentheses.	$= \dfrac{2a}{6} + \dfrac{(3a-3)}{6}$
Place all terms over the common denominator.	$= \dfrac{2a + 3a - 3}{6}$
Collect together like terms.	$= \dfrac{5a - 3}{6}$

Distributive property

The distributive property can be applied to an expression that contains parentheses, in order to remove the parentheses. To apply the distributive property, multiply the term* immediately before the parentheses with every term within them.

e.g. $2(x - 5y) + 5(x + 3y)$
$= 2x - 10y + 5x + 15y$

The expression can then be simplified* by combining the like terms*:

$$2x - 10y + 5x + 15y = 7x + 5y$$

To apply the distributive property to an expression that contains two sets of parentheses, multiply each term in the first set with each term in the second set.

e.g. $(2x + y)(5x - 2y)$
$= [(2x) \times (5x)] + [(2x) \times (^-2y)] + [(y) \times (5x)]$
$+ [(y) \times (^-2y)]$
$= 10x^2 - 4xy + 5xy - 2y^2$

The expression can then be simplified:

$$10x^2 - 4xy + 5xy - 2y^2$$
$$= 10x^2 + xy - 2y^2$$

The same method is used to square* parentheses:

e.g. $(x + a)^2 = (x + a)(x + a)$
$= x^2 + xa + ax + a^2$
$= x^2 + 2ax + a^2$

(Remember, xa and ax are like terms.)

also $(x - a)^2 = (x - a)(x - a)$
$= x^2 - xa - ax + a^2$
$= x^2 - 2ax + a^2$

It is useful to be able to recognize both these squared expressions and their expanded form.

$$(x + a)^2 = x^2 + 2ax + a^2$$
$$(x - a)^2 = x^2 - 2ax + a^2$$

Factoring

When an expression is **factored**, it is rewritten as a product* of its factors*. For example, to factor $5x - 15$, find a common factor* (5) and write it outside a pair of parentheses:

$$5(\quad)$$

Then divide the common factor into each term* $(5x \div 5 = x$ and $^-15 \div 5 = ^-3)$ and write the resulting expression in the parentheses:

$$5x - 15 = 5(x - 3)$$

Check the answer by applying the **distributive property** to the parentheses.

$5(x - 3) = 5x - 15$, so the solution is correct.

To factor a quadratic expression

Quadratic expressions* (containing a squared* number) are factored into two pairs of parentheses. For example, to factor:

$$p^2 + 4p - 12$$

Find a pair of numbers with a product* of $^-12$ and a sum* of 4:

$$(p - 2)(p + 6)$$

This solution is correct because

$^-2 \times 6 = ^-12$ and $^-2 + 6 = 4$
and $(p \times p) + (p \times 6) + (^-2 \times p) + (^-2 \times 6)$
$= p^2 + 6p - 2p - 12 = p^2 + 4p - 12$

Difference between two squares

A binomial expression* involving the subtraction of one **perfect square** from another perfect square (to give the difference). For example, the expression $x^2 - y^2$ is the difference between two squares and can be factored to $(x + y)(x - y)$.

For example, to factor $x^2 - 36$, write down two pairs of parentheses. The first term* in each parentheses is x (the square root* of x^2):

$$(x \quad)(x \quad)$$

The second terms in the parentheses should be the positive and negative square roots of 36:

$$(x + 6)(x - 6)$$

Check the answer by applying the **distributive property**:

$$(x + 6)(x - 6)$$
$$= [(x) \times (x)] + [(x) \times (^-6)] + [6 \times (x)] + [6 \times (^-6)]$$
$$= x^2 - 6x + 6x - 36$$
$$= x^2 - 36$$

Perfect square
A number that is the result of another number (a square root*) multiplied by itself. **Natural* perfect squares** (e.g. $4 \times 4 = 16$) are always integers. **Rational* perfect squares** (e.g. $2.5 \times 2.5 = 6.25$) are not necessarily integers.

---

*Binomial expression 75 (Algebraic expression); Common factor 11; Expression 75; Factor 11; Integers 6; Like terms 75 (Term; Natural number 6; Product 14 (Multiplication); Quadratic expression 85 (Introduction); Rational number 9; Simplification 77; Substitution 77; Sum 14 (Addition); Term, Variable 75.

EQUATIONS

An algebraic **equation** is a mathematical statement that two algebraic expressions* are equal. An equation is solved by finding the value of the unknown variable(s)*. Any value of a variable that satisfies the equation (makes it true) is a **solution**.

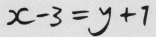

$$x - 3 = y + 1$$

The expressions in an equation are separated by an equals sign (=).

Rearranging an equation

If necessary, the expressions in an equation can be rearranged so that one of the terms* is on its own to the left of the equals sign. The equation can then be solved for that term.

For example, to rearrange this equation and solve for x:
$$4y = 2x - 6$$
Leave the x term on its own by adding 6 to both sides of the equation.
$$4y + 6 = 2x - 6 + 6$$
$$4y + 6 = 2x$$
Next, divide both sides by 2 to give the value of x.
$$\frac{4y + 6}{2} = \frac{2x}{2}$$
$$2y + 3 = x$$
Turn the equation around so that x is on the left.
$$x = 2y + 3$$

If you want to solve for a variable that appears more than once in an equation, you may be able to collect all the terms containing the letter on one side of the equation and then take the letter out as a common factor*. For example, to rearrange this equation and solve for p:
$$\frac{p + q}{r} = \frac{p + r}{q}$$

Multiply both sides by r: $\quad p + q = \dfrac{pr + r^2}{q}$

Multiply both sides by q: $\quad pq + q^2 = pr + r^2$

Take q^2 from both sides: $\quad pq = pr + r^2 - q^2$

Take pr from both sides: $\quad pq - pr = r^2 - q^2$

Factor $pq - pr$: $\quad p(q - r) = r^2 - q^2$

Divide both sides by $q - r$: $\quad p = \dfrac{r^2 - q^2}{q - r}$

Factor $r^2 - q^2$ (the difference of two squares): $\quad p = \dfrac{(r - q)(r + q)}{q - r}$

Cancel like terms
(note, $q - r = -(r - q)$) $\quad p = \dfrac{\overset{-1}{(r - q)}(r + q)}{\underset{1}{q - r}}$

The simplified equation is: $\quad p = {}^-1(r + q)$

Equals sign (=)

This symbol shows that two expressions or values are equal. To maintain this equality, any operation performed on one side of the equals sign must also be performed on the other side.

Solving an equation

If an equation contains just one variable, it can be rearranged and solved for that variable, and the value of the variable can be found. This is called **solving** the equation.

For example, to solve the equation:
$$5x - 3 = 3x + 4$$

Add 3 to both sides: $\quad 5x = 3x + 7$

Subtract 3x from both sides: $\quad 5x - 3x = 3x + 7 - 3x$
$\quad 2x = 7$

Divide both sides by 2: $\quad x = 3.5$

The solution to the equation is $x = 3.5$. You can check this by substitution*.

Trial and improvement

A method of solving problems, such as equations, by trying out different answers to find one that works. You need to be systematic about the numbers you choose. Even so, the solution may be negative, or a fraction or decimal, so this method may take a long time compared with other methods.

For example, to solve the equation $6x + 2 = 20$
Try any number, e.g. 4:
$(6 \times 4) + 2 = 26$ $\quad$ so 4 is too big.

Try a smaller number, e.g. 2.
$(6 \times 2) + 2 = 14$ $\quad$ so 2 is too small.

Try a bigger number, e.g. 3.
$(6 \times 3) + 2 = 20$ $\quad$ so the solution is 3.

ALGEBRAIC GRAPHS

An **algebraic graph** is a drawing that shows the relationship between two or more variables* in an algebraic equation*. The coordinates* of any point on the resulting line or curve satisfy the equation, that is, they make it true.

Drawing a graph

Algebraic graphs are drawn using the Cartesian coordinate system*. When drawing a graph:

① Begin by drawing up a table of values of x and y to give you the coordinates. For example, this is a table of values for the equation $y = \frac{x}{2}$:

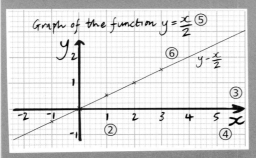

x	-1	0	1	2	3
$y = \frac{x}{2}$	-0.5	0	0.5	1	1.5

*Make sure you have enough points, for example, at least three for a **straight line graph** and more for a curved graph. If necessary, calculate some extra points.*

② Choose an appropriate scale for each axis* and mark it in at suitable intervals. For example, you might choose to make one square represent one unit, or one square represent ten units. If necessary, use a different scale for each axis.

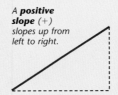

Graph of the function $y = \frac{x}{2}$ ⑤

⑥ $y = \frac{x}{2}$

③ Draw arrows on the end of your axes (to indicate that the lines go on forever).

④ Label the axes (x or y) and, when appropriate, write what they represent and the units in which this is given, e.g. Time (minutes).

⑤ Give your graph a title.

⑥ Plot the coordinates using a cross or dot. Use a sharp pencil and a ruler to join the points on a straight line graph. Always draw curves freehand with the page turned into a position where your wrist is on the inside of the curve. Extend each end of a line or curve to fill the whole of the graph and label the line or curve with the function* used.

General graph terms

Function form
The form of an algebraic equation* that begins "$y = ...$". This form enables you to find the x and y values needed to plot a graph. You can read more about functions on pages 92 to 93.

x-intercept
The point where the line or curve on a graph cuts across the x-axis. At the x-intercept, $y = 0$.

y-intercept
The point where the line or curve on a graph cuts across the y-axis. At the y-intercept, $x = 0$.

Slope (m)
The steepness of a line.

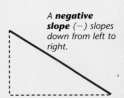

A **positive slope** (+) slopes up from left to right.

A **negative slope** (−) slopes down from left to right.

The slope is the rate at which y increases compared with x between any two points on a line. The bigger the slope, the steeper the line. To find the slope of a line, choose two points on the line, then use the rule:

$$\text{slope} = \frac{y \text{ at B} - y \text{ at A}}{x \text{ at B} - x \text{ at A}}$$

For the line AB, the slope can be calculated by:

$$\frac{7 - 4}{8 - 5}$$
$$= \frac{3}{3}$$
$$= 1$$

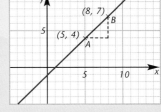

* **Axis** 31 (**Cartesian coordinate system**); **Cartesian coordinate system** 31; **Coefficient** 75; **Coordinates** 31 (**Cartesian coordinates**); **Equations** 79; **Function** 92; **Horizontal, Parallel** 30; **Substitution** 77; **Term** 75; **Variable** 75.

Straight line graphs

In a **straight line**, or **linear**, **graph**, all the points with coordinates that satisfy an equation can be joined together to give a straight line. A **linear equation** can be written in different forms:

Slope/intercept form

The form of the equation for a line
$$y = mx + c$$
where m is the **slope** of the line and c is the y-intercept (where the line crosses the y-axis). For example, the slope of the line $y = 2x + 3$ is 2 and the y-intercept is (0, 3).

Parallel* lines have the same slope, so if the value of m in two equations is identical, then the lines are parallel.

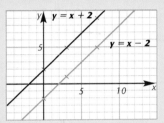

The lines $y = x + 2$ and $y = x - 2$ are parallel as the value of m is the same in both equations (in this case, $m = 1$).

General form

The form of the equation for a line
$$ax + by + c = 0$$
None of the terms* in the general form has particular geometric significance, for example, c does not represent the **y-intercept**.

To convert an equation in general form to slope/intercept form, isolate the y term on one side of the equals sign and divide each term by the coefficient* of y.

e.g. $4x - 2y - 2 = 0$

$^-2y = 2 - 4x$

$y = \dfrac{2 - 4x}{^-2}$

$y = 2x - 1$

Equations in other forms can be converted to slope/intercept form in a similar way.

e.g. $4x - 2 = 2y$

$\dfrac{4x - 2}{2} = \dfrac{2y}{2}$

$2x - 1 = y$

$y = 2x - 1$

To find the equation of a straight line

Use the graph to find the value of m (the **slope**) and c (the **y-intercept**) and substitute* these values in the equation $y = mx + c$.

Sketching a linear graph

A linear equation often contains enough information to allow you to sketch a graph without drawing up a table of values.

The **slope/intercept form** of an equation $y = mx + c$ gives the **slope** (m) and the **y-intercept** (c).

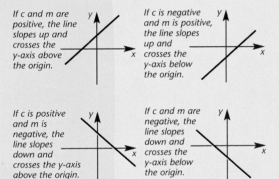

If c and m are positive, the line slopes up and crosses the y-axis above the origin.

If c is negative and m is positive, the line slopes up and crosses the y-axis below the origin.

If c is positive and m is negative, the line slopes down and crosses the y-axis above the origin.

If c and m are negative, the line slopes down and crosses the y-axis below the origin.

If $c = 0$, the equation of a line can be written as $y = mx$. A line with the equation $y = mx$ crosses the y-axis at the origin (where $x = 0$ and $y = 0$), with a slope of m.

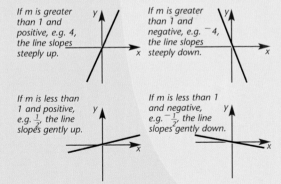

If m is greater than 1 and positive, e.g. 4, the line slopes steeply up.

If m is greater than 1 and negative, e.g. $^-4$, the line slopes steeply down.

If m is less than 1 and positive, e.g. $\frac{1}{2}$, the line slopes gently up.

If m is less than 1 and negative, e.g. $^-\frac{1}{2}$, the line slopes gently down.

If the slope is zero, the line is horizontal*, and is parallel* to the x-axis.

The equation $y = c$ gives a line that is parallel to the x-axis.

To plot a linear graph from an equation*

For example, to plot the linear graph* $y = 2x + 2$:

1. Make a table of x and y values.

x	-4	-3	-2	-1	0	1	2
$y = 2x+2$	-6	-4	-2	0	2	4	6

2. Plot these coordinates* on a graph, and draw a straight line through them.

Graph of the function $y = 2x + 2$

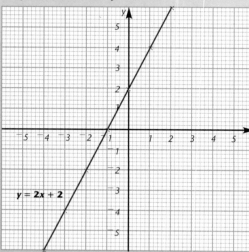

$y = 2x + 2$

3. The solution* to the equation is the point that satisfies the functions* $y = 2x + 2$ and $y = 0$. This is the point at which the line crosses the x-axis. Here, the solution is $x = {}^-1$.

Quadratic graphs

A **quadratic graph** is a drawing of a quadratic expression*. All quadratic graphs can be written in the form:

$$y = ax^2 + bx + c$$

where a, b and c are constants and a is not 0.

Parabola

A "U"-shaped symmetrical* graph. All quadratic functions* produce either positive or negative parabolas, depending on the value of a.

If a is positive, the parabola looks like this.

If a is negative, the parabola looks like this.

Drawing a quadratic graph

As well as following the general guidelines for drawing a graph (see page 80), when drawing a quadratic graph, always show:

- the bottom of the parabola;
- the point where it crosses the x-axis (if it does).

To plot a quadratic graph

Quadratic graphs can be plotted in the same way as other types of graph. For example, to plot the graph of the equation*/function* $y = x^2 + 2x - 4$:

1. Draw a table of values to show the coordinates* of the graph:

x	-4	-3	-2	-1	0	1	2
$y = x^2+2x-4$	4	-1	-4	-5	-4	-1	4

2. Plot these coordinates on a graph and draw a smooth curve through them.

Graph of the function $y = x^2 + 2x - 4$

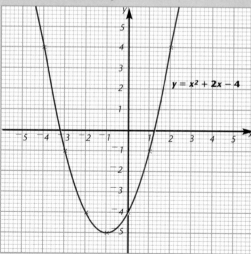

$y = x^2 + 2x - 4$

3. The solutions* to the equation are the points that satisfy the equations $y = x^2 + 2x - 4$ and $y = 0$. These are the points at which the curve crosses the x-axis. Here, the solutions are approximately $x = 1.2$ and $x = {}^-3.2$.

* **Constant** 75; **Coordinate** 31 (**Cartesian coordinates**); **Equation** 79; **Function** 92; **Graph** (**algebraic**) 80; **Linear graph** 81 (**Straight line graphs**); **Quadratic expression** 85 (**Quadratic equations**); **Solution** 79 (**Introduction**); **Symmetry** 42.

Cubic graphs

A **cubic graph** is a drawing of a **cubic expression**, that is, one that contains the term x^3. All cubic graphs can be written in the form:

$$y = ax^3 + bx^2 + cx + d$$

where a, b, c and d are constants* and a is not equal to 0. d is the y-intercept.

The simplest form of cubic graph is $y = x^3$.

Graph of the function $y = x^3$

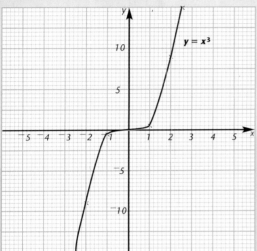

Cubic curve

A curved graph* that has up to two bends in it. The shape of the curve depends on the value of a in the equation $y = ax^3 + bx^2 + cx + d$.

If the value of a is positive, the cubic curve looks similar to 1, 2 and 3.

If the value of a is negative, the cubic curve looks similar to 4, 5 and 6.

1

4

Graphs 1, 2, 4 and 5 have two clear turning points.

2

5

3

Graphs 3 and 6 have two turning points but they are hardly noticeable.

6

To plot a cubic graph

Cubic graphs can be plotted in the same way as other types of graphs.

For example, to plot the graph of the equation* $y = 2x^3 - x^2 - 8x + 4$:

1. Draw a table of values to show the coordinates* of the graph:

x	-2	-1.5	-1	-0.5
$y = 2x^3 - x^2 - 8x + 4$	0	7	9	7.5

x	0	0.5	1	1.5	2
$y = 2x^3 - x^2 - 8x + 4$	4	0	-3	-3.5	0

2. Plot these coordinates on a graph and draw a smooth curve through them.

Graph of the function $y = 2x^3 - x^2 - 8x + 4$

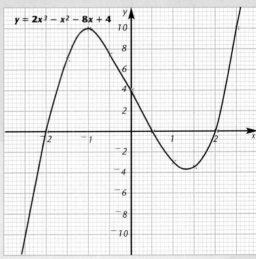

$y = 2x^3 - x^2 - 8x + 4$

3. The solutions* to the cubic equation are the points on the graph that satisfy both the cubic equation and the equation $y = 0$. These are the points at which the curve crosses the x-axis. A cubic equation can have up to three solutions. The solutions to the example above are $x = -2$, $x = 0.5$ and $x = 2$.

Exponential graphs

An **exponential graph** is a drawing of an algebraic expression* in which y is a positive or negative power* of x. All exponential graphs can be written in the form:

$$y = a^x$$

where a is a constant*.

Exponential curve

A graph* representing the function* $y = a^x$. An exponential curve crosses the y-axis where $y = 1$. It does not cross the x-axis. The shape of the curve depends on the value of a.

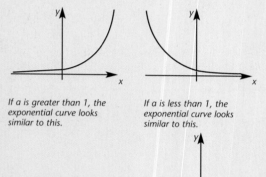

If a is greater than 1, the exponential curve looks similar to this.

If a is less than 1, the exponential curve looks similar to this.

If a is equal to 1, the exponential curve is the horizontal* line $y = 1$.

Reciprocal graphs

All **reciprocal graphs** can be written in the form:

$$y = \frac{a}{x}$$

where a is a constant*.

Hyperbola or reciprocal curve

A graph* consisting of two separate curves that are exact opposites of each other. All reciprocal functions* produce positive or negative hyperbolas, depending on the value of a. If $x = 0$, y does not have a value.

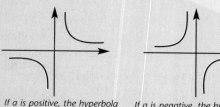

If a is positive, the hyperbola looks similar to this.

If a is negative, the hyperbola looks similar to this.

To plot a reciprocal graph

Reciprocal graphs can be plotted in the same way as any other graphs. For example, to plot the graph of the equation* $y = \frac{6}{x}$, draw a table of values to show the coordinates* of the graph:

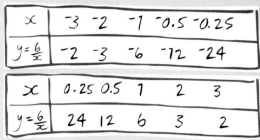

x	⁻3	⁻2	⁻1	⁻0.5	⁻0.25
$y = \frac{6}{x}$	⁻2	⁻3	⁻6	⁻12	⁻24

x	0.25	0.5	1	2	3
$y = \frac{6}{x}$	24	12	6	3	2

Plot these coordinates on a graph and draw two smooth curves through them.

Graph of the function $y = \frac{6}{x}$

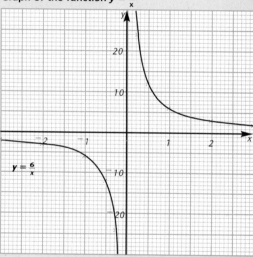

The graph does not cross the x-axis, so cannot be used to solve reciprocal equations.

Circle graphs

An equation* in the form $x^2 + y^2 = r^2$ gives a circle of radius* r and center $(0,0)$.

A graph of the equation $x^2 + y^2 = 4$ looks like this. The radius of the circle is 2 units.

It intersects the x-axis at $(2, 0)$ and $(⁻2, 0)$. It intersects the y-axis at $(0, 2)$ and $(0, ⁻2)$.

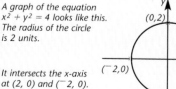

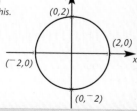

* **Algebraic expression** 75; **Coefficient, Constant** 75; **Coordinates** 31 (**Cartesian coordinates**); **Equation** 79; **Expression (algebraic)** 75; **Factor** 11; **Factoring** 78; **Function** 92; **Graph (algebraic)** 80; **Horizontal** 30; **Power** 21; **Product** 14 (**Multiplication**); **Radius** 65; **Solution** 79 (Introduction); **Squaring** 8 (**Square number**); **Substitution** 77.

QUADRATIC EQUATIONS

A **quadratic equation** is an equation* that includes a **quadratic expression***, that is, a variable that is squared*. Quadratic equations can be written in the form $ax^2 + bx + c = 0$, where a does not equal 0. Every quadratic equation that can be solved has two solutions*, called **roots**. Quadratic equations can also be solved using a graph (see page 82), or using the methods described below and on page 86.

$$x^2 - 2x - 5 = 5$$

$$2x^2 + 6x + 4 = 0$$

These equations are both quadratic equations because they can be written in the form $y = ax^2 + bx + c$.

Solving by factoring

This method involves factoring* the equation to give two expressions* in parentheses. Since $ax^2 + bx + c = 0$, one of the expressions in parentheses must be equal to 0 (as the result of multiplying any value by 0 is 0). By taking each parenthesis at a time, the two possible solutions to the equation can be found. Not all quadratic equations can be solved by factoring.

1. Factor the left side of the equation to give two expressions in parentheses. First find two factors* of the x term. Then find two numbers which, when multiplied, are equal to c (the coefficient* of x) and when added are equal to b (the constant*).
   e.g. $x^2 + 6x + 8 = 0$
   $(x + 2) (x + 4) = 0$
   (The x values are correct because $x \times x = x^2$, and the numbers are correct because $2 + 4 = 6$ and $2 \times 4 = 8$.)

2. Since the product* of the factors is 0, one of the factors must equal 0. Calculate the value of x for each pair of parentheses.
   e.g. if $(x + 2) (x + 4) = 0$
   then either $(x + 2) = 0$ or $(x + 4) = 0$
   so either $x = {}^-2$ or $x = {}^-4$

   The roots of the quadratic equation $x^2 + 6x + 8 = 0$ are $x = {}^-2$ and $x = {}^-4$.

3. Check your answer by substituting* each root in turn into the original equation.
   e.g.   (when $x = {}^-2$) $4 + {}^-12 + 8 = 0$
   (when $x = {}^-4$) $16 + {}^-24 + 8 = 0$ ✓

Identifying factors
If the coefficient* of x^2 is greater than 1 (that is, $2x^2$, $3x^2$, $4x^2$ ...), it can be difficult to know the correct way to factor the equation without trying several alternatives.

For example, to factor the equation $4x^2 + 20x + 21 = 0$, the coefficients of x must multiply to give 4, and the numbers must add up to 20 and multiply to give 21.

$(4x + 3) (x + 7) = 4x^2 + 28x + 3x + 21$
$\qquad\qquad\qquad = 4x^2 + 31x + 21$ ✗

$(4x + 7) (x + 3) = 4x^2 + 12x + 7x + 21$
$\qquad\qquad\qquad = 4x^2 + 19x + 21$ ✗

$(2x + 3) (2x + 7) = 4x^2 + 14x + 6x + 21$
$\qquad\qquad\qquad\quad = 4x^2 + 20x + 21$ ✓

Once you have the correct factor, you can find the roots of the equation.
e.g. $2x + 3 = 0$
$2x = 0 - 3$
$2x = {}^-3$
$x = {}^-1.5$

$2x + 7 = 0$
$2x = 0 - 7$
$2x = {}^-7$
$x = {}^-3.5$

The roots of the equation $4x^2 + 20x + 21 = 0$ are $x = {}^-1.5$ and $x = {}^-3.5$.

Check your answer by substituting* each root in turn into the original equation.
e.g.   (when $x = {}^-1.5$) $9 + {}^-30 + 21 = 0$
(when $x = {}^-3.5$) $49 + {}^-70 + 21 = 0$ ✓

Completing the square

$$(x+3)^2 = 9$$
$$(x-5)^2 = 11$$

Any equation* in the form
$(x + y)^2 = z$ is a perfect square*.

Completing the square means making the left-hand side of a quadratic equation* into a perfect square*, resulting in the form $(x + y)^2 = z$. This method can be used to solve any quadratic equation.

1. Make sure that the equation is in the form $ax^2 + bx + c = 0$. Then move the number (c) to the right-hand side of the equation.

   For example, to solve the quadratic equation $x^2 - 6x + 2 = 0$, first move the 2 to the right-hand side of the equation:
   e.g. $x^2 - 6x = {}^-2$

2. To complete the square on the left-hand side, halve the coefficient* of x and square* the result, then add this number to both sides.
   e.g. $\left(\dfrac{6}{2}\right)^2 = (3)^2 = 9$
   so: $x^2 - 6x + 9 = {}^-2 + 9$
   $x^2 - 6x + 9 = 7$

3. Factor* the left-hand side of the equation in the form $(x + y)^2 = z$.
   e.g. $x^2 - 6x + 9 = 7$
   $(x - 3)^2 = 7$

4. Find the square root* of both sides to find the roots* of the equation.
   e.g. $(x - 3)^2 = 7$
   $x - 3 = \pm\sqrt{7}$
   $x = \pm 2.645\,751\,31 + 3$

   so: $x = 5.645\,751\,31$ or $x = 0.354\,248\,69$

5. Round* your final answer to an appropriate degree of accuracy.
   e.g. $x = 5.65$ (3 s.f.)
   or $x = 0.354$ (3 s.f.)

The quadratic formula

The **quadratic formula** can be used to solve any equation in the form $ax^2 + bx + c = 0$. The quadratic formula is:
$$x = \frac{{}^-b \pm \sqrt{b^2 - 4ac}}{2a}$$

1. Make sure that the equation is in the form $ax^2 + bx + c = 0$ and identify a, b and c.
   e.g. $2x^2 + 4x - 6 = 0$
   in which case, $a = 2$, $b = 4$ and $c = {}^-6$

2. Solve the equation by substituting* the values for a, b and c into the quadratic formula.
   e.g. $x = \dfrac{{}^-4 \pm \sqrt{4^2 - 4 \times 2 \times {}^-6}}{2 \times 2}$

   $x = \dfrac{{}^-4 \pm \sqrt{16 + 48}}{4}$

   $x = \dfrac{{}^-4 \pm \sqrt{64}}{4}$

   $x = \dfrac{{}^-4 + \sqrt{64}}{4}$ or $x = \dfrac{{}^-4 - \sqrt{64}}{4}$

   $x = \dfrac{{}^-4 + 8}{4}$ or $x = \dfrac{{}^-4 - 8}{4}$

   $x = \dfrac{4}{4}$ or $x = \dfrac{{}^-12}{4}$

   $x = 1$ or $x = {}^-3$

   The roots* of the equation $2x^2 + 4x - 6 = 0$ are $x = 1$ and $x = {}^-3$.

4. Check your answer. If it is correct, the sum* of the roots should be $\dfrac{{}^-b}{a}$.

   e.g. $1 + {}^-3 = {}^-2$ and $\dfrac{{}^-b}{a} = \dfrac{{}^-4}{2} = {}^-2$ ✓

This checking method works because the quadratic formula gives the two values of x as

$$\dfrac{{}^-b}{2a} + \dfrac{b^2 - 4ac}{2a} \quad \text{and} \quad \dfrac{{}^-b}{2a} - \dfrac{b^2 - 4ac}{2a}$$

The sum of these two roots is:

$$\left(\dfrac{{}^-b}{2a}\right) + \left(\dfrac{b^2 - 4ac}{2a}\right) + \left(\dfrac{{}^-b}{2a}\right) - \left(\dfrac{b^2 - 4ac}{2a}\right)$$

$$= \left(\dfrac{{}^-b}{2a}\right) + \left(\dfrac{{}^-b}{2a}\right) = \dfrac{{}^-2b}{2a} = \dfrac{{}^-}{}$$

* **Coefficient** 75; **Equation** 79; **Expression (algebraic)** 75; **Factoring** 78; **Like terms** 75 (**Term**); **Perfect square** 78; **Quadratic equation** 85; **Rearranging an equation** 79; **Root** 85; **Rounding** 16; **Simplifying** 77 (**Simplification**); **Square root** 11; **Squaring** 8 (**Square number**); **Substitution** 77; **Sum** 14 (**Addition**); **Term** 75; **Variable** 75.

SIMULTANEOUS EQUATIONS

Simultaneous equations are pairs of equations* in which the variables* represent the same numbers in each equation. To solve simultaneous equations, you must find a solution that satisfies both equations (makes them both true).

$$3x + y = 8$$
$$x + y = 4$$

These equations can be solved together to give values of x and y that make both equations true. In this case, the value of both x and y is 2.

Solving by substitution

By substituting* one of the expressions* into the other equation, the value of one variable can be found. This value can then be substituted into the first equation to find the remaining variable.

1. If necessary, rearrange* one of the equations to solve for the variable.
    For example, to solve the equations:
    $$5x - y = 13$$
    $$2x + y = 15$$
    rearrange the first equation to solve for y:
    $$y = 5x - 13$$

2. Substitute the rewritten expression for the same variable in the other equation.
    e.g. If $y = 5x - 13$
    $2x + y = 15$ can be rewritten as
    $$2x + 5x - 13 = 15$$

3. Collect like terms* on one side and simplify*.
    e.g. $2x + 5x - 13 = 15$
    $$7x - 13 = 15$$
    $$7x = 15 + 13$$
    $$7x = 28$$
    $$x = 4$$

4. Substitute the value of the known variable into the remaining equation and use it to find the value of the other variable.
    e.g. $x = 4$, so $(2 \times 4) + y = 15$
    $$8 + y = 15$$
    $$y = 15 - 8$$
    $$y = 7$$
    The solution is $x = 4$ and $y = 7$.

5. Check your answer by substituting the x and y values into the other equation.
    e.g. $20 - 7 = 13$, so the answer is correct. ✓

Solving by elimination

If the same or opposite terms* appear in both equations, they can be combined to **eliminate** that term, leaving only one variable. The equation can then be simplified* to give the value of the variable, which can then be substituted* into either of the equations to find the other unknown variable.

To eliminate terms that are the same or opposite
1. If the terms are the same (e.g. $2x$ and $2x$ or ^-2x and ^-2x), subtract one equation from the other. If the terms are opposite (e.g. $2x$ and ^-2x), add the equations.
    For example, to solve the equations:
    $$2x - 3y = 5$$
    $$x + 3y = 16$$
    add the terms together (as opposite like terms* appear in both equations):
    $$(2x - 3y) + (x + 3y) = 5 + 16$$
    $$3x = 21$$
    $$x = 7$$

2. Substitute the value of the known variable into either of the equations. The value of the remaining variable can then be found.
    e.g. $2x - 3y = 5$
    $$(2 \times 7) - 3y = 5$$
    $$14 - 3y = 5$$
    $$3y = 14 - 5$$
    $$3y = 9$$
    $$y = 3$$
    The solution is $x = 7$ and $y = 3$.

3. Check your answer by substituting the x and y values into the other equation.
    e.g. $7 + 9 = 16$, so the answer is correct. ✓

Elimination continued

To eliminate* like terms* if their coefficients* are not equal or opposite

1. Find the least common multiple* of one pair of coefficients (that is, the x values or the y values) and multiply one or both equations* by the required number to make those coefficients equal.

For example, to solve the simultaneous equations:
$$2x + 3y = 0$$
$$3x + 2y = 5$$
multiply the first equation by 2 and the second equation by 3:
$$4x + 6y = 0$$
$$9x + 6y = 15$$

(Alternatively, here you could multiply the first equation by 3 and the second by 2 to make both the x values 6x.)

2. If the terms* are the same (e.g. 2x and 2x or ⁻2x and ⁻2x), subtract one equation from the other. If the terms are opposite (e.g. 2x and ⁻2x), add the equations.
e.g. $(4x + 6y) - (9x + 6y) = 0 - 15$
$$⁻5x = ⁻15$$
$$5x = 15$$
$$x = 3$$

3. Substitute* the value of the known variable* into either of the equations. The value of the remaining equation can then be found.
e.g. $4 \times 3 + 6y = 0$
$$12 + 6y = 0$$
$$6y = ⁻12$$
$$y = ⁻2$$
The solution is $x = 3$ and $y = ⁻2$.

4. Check your answer by substituting the x and y values into the original equations.
e.g.
$$6 - 6 = 0 \qquad ✓$$
and
$$9 - 4 = 5 \qquad ✓$$

$6 - 6 = 0$ and $9 - 4 = 5$, so the answer is correct.

Solving with a graph

Simultaneous equations* can be represented by graphs. (You can read more about the different types of graphs on pages 82 to 86.) Each line or curve on the graph represents an equation and the point where the two lines cross provides an x and y value which satisfies both equations.

To plot a graph of simultaneous linear equations

For example, to plot the graph of the simultaneous equations:
$$x - 1 = y$$
$$2y + 2x = 6$$
rearrange* the equations to solve for y:
$$y = x - 1$$
$$y = 3 - x$$
For each equation, make a table showing possible values of x and y.

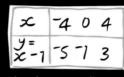

x	⁻4	0	4
$y = x-1$	⁻5	⁻1	3

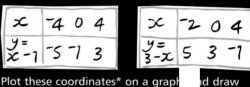

x	⁻2	0	4
$y = 3-x$	5	3	⁻1

Plot these coordinates* on a graph and draw a line through each set. Label each line with its equation.

Graph of the functions $y = x - 1$ and $y = 3 - x$

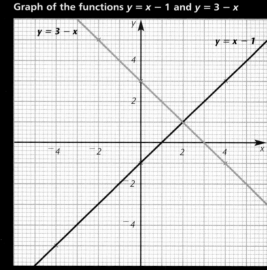

In this example, the lines $y = x - 1$ and $y = 3 - x$ meet at the point (2, 1). So, the solution to the simultaneous equations is $x = 2$ and $y = 1$.

*Coefficient 75; Completing the square 86; Coordinates 31 (Cartesian coordinates); Elimination 87 (Solving by elimination); Equation 79; Factoring 78; Least common multiple 11 (Common multiple); Like terms 75 (Term); Quadratic formula 86; Rearranging the equation 79; Simplifying 77; Simultaneous equations 87; Substituting 77; Term, Variable 75.

More simultaneous equations

Linear and quadratic equations*

For example to solve:
$$y = x + 3 \qquad (1)$$
$$y = x^2 - 4x + 7 \qquad (2)$$
Substitute* the y value from equation (1) into equation (2) and simplify*:
$$x + 3 = x^2 - 4x + 7$$
$$3 = x^2 - 4x + 7 - x$$
$$3 = x^2 - 5x + 7$$
$$0 = x^2 - 5x + 4$$
$$x^2 - 5x + 4 = 0$$
Factor* the equation, then solve it to find x.
$$(x - 1)(x - 4) = 0$$
either $x - 1 = 0$ or $x - 4 = 0$
so $x = 1$ or $x = 4$

Substitute the x values into equation (1):
When $x = 1$: $y = 1 + 3$, so $y = 4$
When $x = 4$: $y = 4 + 3$, so $y = 7$

Check the answer by substituting both values into equation (2):
$4 = 1 - 4 + 7$ ✓ and $7 = 16 - 16 + 7$ ✓

If the equations cannot be factored, try completing the square* or using the quadratic formula*. You can also solve simultaneous equations using a graph. The coordinates* of the points where the graphs cross one another provide the solutions.

Graph of the functions $y = x + 3$ and $y = x^2 - 4x + 7$

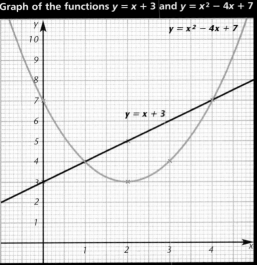

Linear and circle equations

For example to solve:
$$y = x - 1 \qquad (1)$$
$$x^2 + y^2 = 25 \qquad (2)$$
Substitute* the y value from equation* (1) into equation (2) and simplify:
$$x^2 + (x - 1)^2 = 25$$
$$x^2 + (x - 1)(x - 1) = 25$$
$$x^2 + x^2 - x - x + 1 = 25$$
$$2x^2 - 2x + 1 = 25$$
$$2x^2 - 2x - 24 = 0$$
Factor* the equation, then solve it to find x.
$$(2x + 6)(x - 4) = 0$$
either $2x + 6 = 0$ or $x - 4 = 0$
so $x = {}^-3$ or $x = 4$

Substitute the x values into equation (1):
When $x = {}^-3$: $y = {}^-3 - 1$, so $y = {}^-4$
When $x = 4$: $y = 4 - 1$, so $y = 3$

Check the answer by substituting both values into the second equation (2):
$({}^-3)^2 + ({}^-4)^2 = 25$ and $4^2 + 3^2 = 25$
$9 + 16 = 25$ ✓ $16 + 9 = 25$ ✓

If the equations cannot be factored, try completing the square*, using the quadratic formula* or drawing a graph. The coordinates* of the points where the graphs cross provide the solution to the simultaneous equations. Remember that an equation in the form $x^2 + y^2 = r^2$ gives a circle with its center at the origin (0, 0) and radius r (see *Circle graphs* on page 84).

Graph of the functions $y = x - 1$ and $x^2 + y^2 = 25$

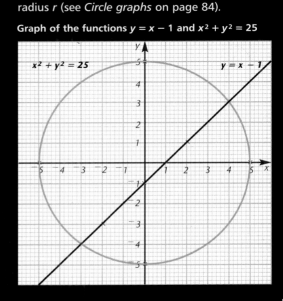

INEQUALITIES

An **inequality** is a mathematical statement that two algebraic expressions* are not equal. An inequality is the opposite of an equation*, but can be solved in a similar way, to give a range of values that satisfy the inequality (make it true).

$$2x + 3 < 8$$

The expressions in an inequality are separated by an inequality sign. There are several signs with different meanings. The sign in this inequality means "is less than."

Inequality notation

The symbols used to indicate an inequality. These include:

$<$ means "less than"

$>$ means "greater than"

$\leqslant$ means "less than or equal to"

$\geqslant$ means "greater than or equal to"

$\neq$ means "not equal to"

For example, $x < y$ means that x is less than y, and $a \geqslant b$ means that a is greater than or equal to b. (You may find it useful to remember that the sign for "**Less than**" ($<$) looks like a tilted capital letter "**L**".)

Inequalities can be rearranged*, but the inequality sign must be reversed. For example if x is less then y ($x < y$) then y must be greater than x ($y > x$). Similarly, if a is more than or equal to b ($a \geqslant b$), b must be less than or equal to a ($b \leqslant a$).

Inequalities can be shown on a number line*. Values that are included in an inequality are indicated by a filled circle. A value is included when the variable* is $\leqslant$ or $\geqslant$ the value.

This number line shows the inequality $x \geqslant 1$. The value 1 is included in the inequality, so it is represented by a filled circle.

Values that are not included in an inequality are indicated by an open circle. A value is not included when the variable* is $<$ or $>$ the value.

This number line shows the inequality $^-2 < x < 6$. The values $^-2$ and 6 are not included in the inequality, so they are represented by open circles.

Conditional inequality

An inequality that is true only for certain values of the variables*, for example $x + 1 \geqslant 4$, which is only true for values of $x \geqslant 3$.

Unconditional inequality

An inequality that is true for all values of the variables*, e.g. $x + 1 > x - 1$.

Double inequality

An inequality in which a variable* has to satisfy two inequalities. For example, in the double inequality $0 \leqslant x \leqslant 5$, x must be greater than or equal to 0 and also be less than or equal to 5.

Solving single inequalities

Inequalities can be solved in a similar way to equations, by rearranging* the inequality and solving for an unknown variable. To keep the inequality true, any term* added or subtracted on one side of the inequality must be added or subtracted on the other side. Similarly, if you multiply or divide one side of an inequality by a positive term, you must do the same to the other side. However, if you multiply or divide both sides by a negative number, you also need to reverse the inequality sign.

For example, to solve the inequality:
$$4 - 3y \geqslant 12 - y$$
Subtract 4 from both sides: $\quad ^-3y \geqslant 12 - y - 4$

Add y to both sides: $\quad ^-3y + y \geqslant 12 - 4$

$$^-2y \geqslant 8$$

Divide both sides by $^-2$ and reverse the inequality sign: $\quad y \leqslant ^-4$

The solution to the inequality is $y \leqslant ^-4$.

This solution can be illustrated on a number line:

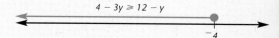

$4 - 3y \geqslant 12 - y$

* **Algebraic expression** 75; **Coordinates** 31 (**Cartesian coordinates**); **Equation** 79; **Graph (algebraic)** 80;
Linear equation 81 (Introduction); **Number line** 7 (**Directed numbers**); **Rearranging an equation** 79;
Substitution 77; **Term** 75; **Variable** 75; **Vertices (Vertex)** 34 (**Polygons**).

Solving double inequalities

A **double inequality** represents two inequalities, so for example, $5 \geqslant 2x + 3 \geqslant x + 1$ represents the inequalities: $5 \geqslant 2x + 3$ and $2x + 3 \geqslant x + 1$.

To find a solution that satisfies both inequalities, solve each inequality in turn:

$5 \geqslant 2x + 3$	$2x + 3 \geqslant x + 1$
$5 - 3 \geqslant 2x$	$2x - x + 3 \geqslant 1$
$2 \geqslant 2x$	$x \geqslant 1 - 3$
$1 \geqslant x$	$x \geqslant {}^-2$

Values of x that are greater than or equal to $^-2$ and less than or equal to 1 satisfy both inequalities. These solutions can be expressed by the double inequality $^-2 \leqslant x \leqslant 1$ and can be illustrated on a number line:

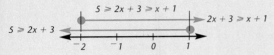

Graphs of inequalities

An inequality can be represented by a region on a graph*. To plot a graph of an inequality:

1. Replace the inequality sign with an equals sign ($=$) and plot the resulting equation on a graph. (You can find out more about plotting graphs on page 80.) For example, to show the inequality $x \leqslant 4$, first plot coordinates* that satisfy the linear equation* $x = 4$.

2. Join the points with a solid or dotted line. A solid line shows that points on it are included in the inequality (this is indicated by the symbols $\leqslant$ or $\geqslant$ in the inequality). A dotted line shows that the points on it are not included (this is indicated by the symbols $<$ or $>$ in the inequality).

3. Unless asked to do otherwise, shade the region that is included. Always clearly label the region that is included in the inequality.

4. If you need to find a range of values that satisfy more than one inequality, draw a line for each inequality and then shade out and label the required region.

Example: Inequality problem

Find the region defined by the inequalities $y < 2 - x$, $x \geqslant {}^-4$ and $y \geqslant x - 1$. Use your graph to find the points with coordinates* where the values of $3x + y$ are a) greatest and b) least.

Make a table of x and y values for the equations $y = 2 - x$ and $y = x - 1$ then plot each set of coordinates on a graph and draw straight lines through them. Shade the included regions.

x	$^-4$	$^-2$	0	2	4
$y = 2 - x$	6	4	2	0	$^-2$

x	$^-3$	$^-1$	1	3	5
$y = x - 1$	$^-4$	$^-2$	0	2	4

Graph of the functions $y < 2 - x$, $x \geqslant {}^-4$ and $y \geqslant x - 1$

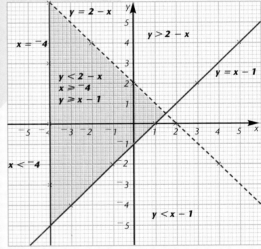

The unshaded region is defined by the inequalities $y < 2 - x$, $x \geqslant {}^-4$ and $y \geqslant x - 1$.

The x and y values at the vertices* of the region are at their highest or lowest while still satisfying the inequalities. To find the greatest and least values of an equation, substitute* the coordinates of each vertex in turn into the equation and compare the answers.

At $(^-4, {}^-5)$	$3x + y = {}^-12 + {}^-5 = {}^-17$
At $(^-4, 6)$	$3x + y = {}^-12 + 6 = {}^-6$
At $(1.5, 0.5)$	$3x + y = 4.5 + 0.5 = 5$

a) The value of $3x + y$ is greatest at $(1.5, 0.5)$.
b) The value of $3x + y$ is least at $(^-4, {}^-5)$.

Internet links For links to useful websites on **inequalities**, go to *www.usborne-quicklinks.com*

FUNCTIONS

A **function** is a rule that is applied to one set* of values to give another set of values. Each value in the first set is related to only one value in the second. Rules such as "double," "square" and "add 1" are all functions. A function is represented by the letter f.

Result

The value that is obtained when a function is applied to a value x. The result is represented by $f(x)$, which is said, "f of x." For example, if f is the function "add 1," $f(x) = x + 1$. A function can be applied to any value of x so, when $f(x) = x + 1$, $f(2) = 2 + 1 = 3$ and $f(200) = 200 + 1 = 201$. The set of results is called the **image of f** and it is a subset* of the **range**.

Domain

The set* of values to which a function is applied.

Range

The set* of values to which the **results** belong. Often this is the entire set of real numbers*.

Composite function

A combination of two or more functions. This can be written as $f \circ g(x)$, where function g is done first, or $g \circ f(x)$, where function f is done first. For example, if $f(x) = x^2$ and $g(x) = 3x - 1$,
$$f \circ g(x) = f(3x - 1) = (3x - 1)^2.$$
and $\quad g \circ f(x) = g(x^2) = 3x^2 - 1$

Inverse function

An operation or series of operations that reverses a function. This is usually written $f^{-1}(x)$. For example, to find the inverse of the function $f(x) = 3x + 5$:

1. Let $y = f(x)$: $\qquad\qquad y = 3x + 5$
2. Swap all x and y variables: $\quad x = 3y + 5$
3. Rearrange* to solve for y: $\quad 3y = x - 5$
$$y = \frac{x - 5}{3}$$
4. Let $y = f^{-1}(x)$ $\qquad\qquad f^{-1}(x) = \frac{x - 5}{3}$

Map or mapping

Another name for a function. Mapping notation is different from function notation, and uses the symbol $\mapsto$, which means "maps to." For example, in mapping notation "$f(x) = 2x$" is "$f : x \mapsto 2x$."

Illustrating functions

There are several ways to illustrate a function: set notation, number lines, a flow chart or a graph*.

Set notation

Each element* of the **domain** corresponds with an element in the **range**.
e.g.
for $f(x) = 2x$

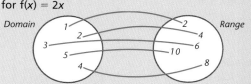

Number lines

The number line on the left below represents the **domain**, and the one on the right represents the **range**. Each value in the domain corresponds with a value in the range.
e.g.
for $f(x) = x + 1$

Flow chart or flow diagram

Diagram showing the order of operations to find the value of a function. The rounded frames show the value at the start and end of each calculation and the rectangular boxes contain the functions.

This flow chart illustrates the function $f(x) = 3x + 1$.

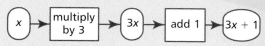

*To find the **inverse function**, read the flow chart from right to left and reverse each operation. For example, the function above $f(x) = 3x + 1$, has the inverse $f^{-1}(x) = \frac{x - 1}{3}$.*

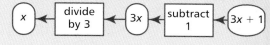

* **Constant** 75; **Cosine** 60 (Introduction); **Element** 12; **Graph (algebraic)** 80; **Radius** 65; **Real numbers** 9; **Rearranging an equation** 79; **Scale factor** 52; **Set** 12; **Sine** 60 (Introduction); **Subset** 12; **Tangent** 60 (Introduction); **x-axis, y-axis** 31 (**Cartesian coordinate system**).

Functions and graphs

Functions can be shown on a graph*, with the **domain** on the *x*-axis* and the **range** on the *y*-axis*. The *y*-axis can be labeled either "*y*" or "f(*x*)," since *y* = f(*x*). If you label the *y*-axis "*y*," label the graph "*y* = ..." If you label the *y*-axis "f(*x*)," label the graph "f(*x*) = ..." (see below).

Each of the functions described below gives a characteristic graph. You can see examples of these graphs on pages 81–84 and page 64.

Graph of f(x) = x − 1

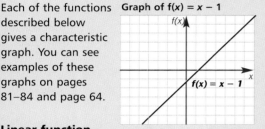

Linear function
Any function in the form f(*x*) = *mx* + *c* (where *m* is not equal to 0). (See graphs on pages 81–82.)

Quadratic function
Any function in the form f(*x*) = *ax*² + *bx* + *c* (where *a*, *b* and *c* are constants* and *a* is not equal to 0). (See graph on page 82.)

Cubic function
Any function in the form f(*x*) = *ax*³ + *bx*² + *cx* + *d* (where *a*, *b*, *c* and *d* are constants* and *a* is not equal to 0). (See graphs on page 83.)

Exponential function
Any function in the form f(*x*) = *a*ˣ (where *a* is a constant*). (See graphs on page 84.)

Reciprocal function
Any function in the form f(*x*) = $\frac{a}{x}$ (where *a* is a constant*). (See graphs on page 84.)

Circle function
Any function that can be written in the form f(*x*) = $\sqrt{(x-a)^2 + (y-b)^2}$ where (*a*, *b*) are the coordinates of the center of the circle. The graph on page 84 shows a simple example, in the form *x*² + *y*² = *r*², which gives a circle of radius* *r* and center (0,0).

Trigonometric, or circular, function
A function in the form f(*x*) = sine* *x*, f(*x*) = cosine* *x* or f(*x*) = tangent* *x*. (See graphs on page 64.)

Transformation of graphs

If the graph* of a function is plotted, that graph can then be transformed by altering the function. For example, if you replace f(*x*) with ⁻f(*x*), the graph is reflected in the *x*-axis, and if you replace f(*x*) with f(⁻*x*), the graph is reflected in the *y*-axis. Below are four other common graph transformations.

Transformation y = f(x + a)

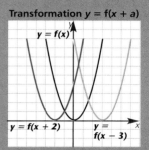

The transformation *y* = f(*x* + *a*) translates (moves) the graph along the *x*-axis. If *a* > 0, the graph moves to the left (negative direction). If *a* < 0, it moves to the right (positive direction).

Transformation y = f(x) + a

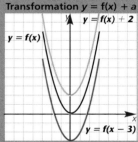

The transformation *y* = f(*x*) + *a* translates (moves) the graph along the *y*-axis. If *a* < 0, the graph moves down the *y*-axis (negative direction). If *a* > 0, it moves up the *y*-axis (positive direction).

Transformation y = af(x)

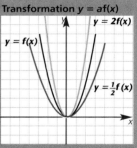

The transformation *y* = *a*f(*x*) stretches or shrinks that graph along the *y*-axis, with a scale factor* of *a*. If *a* > 1, the graph stretches along the *y*-axis. If if *a* < 1, it shrinks along the *y*-axis.

Transformation y = f(ax)

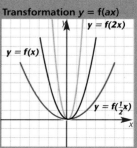

The transformation *y* = f(*ax*) shrinks or stretches the graph along the *x*-axis, with a scale factor* of $\frac{1}{a}$. If *a* > 1, the graph shrinks along the *x*-axis. If *a* < 1, the graph stretches along the *x*-axis.

INFORMATION FROM GRAPHS

Since a graph is an illustration of the relationship between two quantities, it can be used to find the value on the *y*-axis* that corresponds with any given value on the *x*-axis*, and vice versa. In addition, both the area* under a graph, and the slope* of a graph can provide further information about the quantities it represents.

The area under a graph

If the units of measurement used on the *x*- and *y*-axes are known, the area under a graph gives a third unit of measurement. Whatever the shape of the region under the graph, the formula* for finding its area involves multiplying distances along the axes. For this reason, the area under a graph can be expressed by the general rule:

$$\text{area under a graph} = \text{units along the } x\text{-axis} \times \text{units along the } y\text{-axis}$$

For example, on a **speed-time graph** (a graph showing the rate of speed against time) like the one below, the *y*-axis shows speed (distance divided by time) and the *x*-axis shows time.

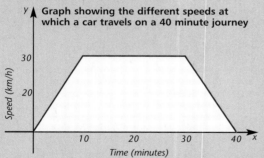

Graph showing the different speeds at which a car travels on a 40 minute journey

If these quantities are substituted* into the general formula for the area under the graph, the rewritten formula is:

$$\text{area under graph} = \text{time} \times \frac{\text{distance}}{\text{time}}$$

$$\text{area under graph} = \text{distance}$$

So, the area under a speed-time graph gives a value for the distance traveled.

You can use this method to find the meaning of the area under graphs showing other quantities. For example, if the *x*-axis represents density* (mass* divided by volume*) and the *y*-axis represents volume, the area under the graph gives the mass.

To find the area under a straight graph

Use the appropriate formula for the shape of the area to be found. For example, the graph below represents the speed of a car on a journey. What was the total distance covered?

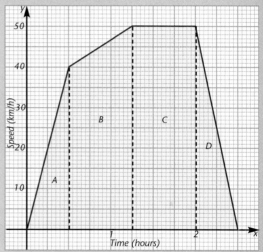

Graph of the speed of a car

Divide the area up into separate shapes and find the area of each shape.

Area of triangle A:
$\frac{1}{2} \times \text{base} \times \text{height} = \frac{1}{2} \times 0.5 \times 40 = 10\text{km}$

Area of trapezoid* B
$\frac{1}{2} \times (\text{sum* of parallel sides}) \times \text{distance between them}$
$= \frac{1}{2} \times (40 + 50) \times 0.75 = \frac{1}{2} \times 90 \times 0.75 = 33.75\text{k}$

Area of rectangle C:
$\text{length} \times \text{width} = 0.75 \times 50 = 37.5\text{km}$

Area of triangle C:
$\frac{1}{2} \times \text{base} \times \text{height} = \frac{1}{2} \times 0.5 \times 50 = 12.5\text{km}$

Total $= 10 + 33.75 + 37.5 + 12.5 = 93.75\text{km}$

The total distance covered was 93.75km.

To find the area under a curved graph

Divide the area under the curve into a convenient number of vertical* strips, preferably an equal distance apart, and draw a chord* across the top of each strip to form a row of trapezoids*. The sum* of the areas of these trapezoids will give an approximate value for the area under the curve. This method is called the **trapezoid rule**. The narrower the trapezoids, the better the approximation will be.

If the trapezoids are all the same width, you can find their combined area using:

$$\text{area} = \tfrac{1}{2} \times w \times (\text{first} + \text{last} + 2(\text{sum of rest}))$$

where w is the distance between the sides of the trapezoids, "first" is the height of the left-hand side of the first trapezoid, "last" is the height of the right-hand side of the last trapezoid and "the rest" is the sides of all the trapezoids in between.

For example, the speed-time graph below shows the motion of a clockwork mouse. Approximately how far does the mouse travel in 40 seconds?

Graph showing the speed of a clockwork mouse

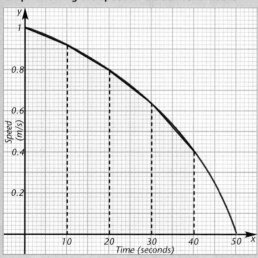

$$\tfrac{1}{2} \times 10 \times (1 + 0.4 + (2 \times (0.92 + 0.8 + 0.64)))$$
$$= 5 \times (1.4 + 4.72)$$
$$= 5 \times 6.12 = 30.6m$$

The clockwork mouse travels 30.6m in 40 seconds.

If the area under a graph is divided into trapezoids of unequal widths, calculate the area of each one separately, then add them together.

Gradients and tangents

Finding the slope* of a graph involves dividing the distance along the y-axis by the distance along the x-axis. As a result of this, a graph's slope can give further information about the relationship between the quantities illustrated by the graph. The table below shows examples of information a slope can provide.

y quantity	x quantity	slope shows
displacement*	time	velocity*
velocity	time	acceleration*
mass*	volume*	density*

The slope of a straight line can be found by dividing the vertical* distance between two points on the line by the horizontal* distance between the points (see page 80). The slope of a curve varies and can only be found for a given point. This is done by drawing a tangent* at that point and finding the slope of the tangent.

For example, to find the slope at point $x = 2$ of the curve $y = x^2 + 3$, draw a tangent to the curve at the point $x = 2$. To draw the tangent, place your ruler at $x = 2$ and tilt it until the angles between the curve and the ruler on either side of the point look equal, then draw a line.

Graph of the function $y = x^2 + 3$

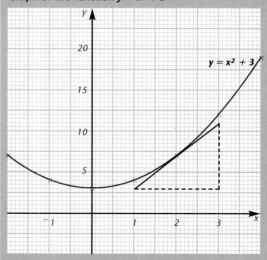

To find the slope of the tangent use:

$$\frac{\text{units along the } y\text{-axis}}{\text{units along the } x\text{-axis}} = \frac{8}{2} = 4$$

So, the slope of the graph $y = x^2 + 3$ at $x = 2$ is 4.

Internet links For links to useful websites on **algebraic graphs**, go to www.usborne-quicklinks.com

DATA

Data is the collective name for pieces of information. (The singular is **datum**: it is not often used.) The branch of math concerned with collecting, recording, interpreting, illustrating and analyzing large amounts of data is known as **statistics**.

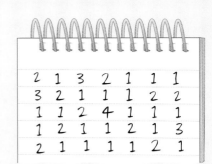

This data list shows the number of people in each car that passed a school's gates between 10am and 10:15am on one day. The data is **raw**: it has not yet been sorted.*

Types of data

Quantitative data

Information about quantities that can be measured using numbers. Measurements such as length*, mass* and speed* are examples of quantitative data.

Qualitative data or categorical data

Information about qualities that cannot be measured using numbers. Colors, scents, tastes and shapes are examples of qualitative data.

Discrete data

Information that can be expressed only by a specific value, such as in whole or half numbers. The number of people in a group is an example of discrete data because people can only be counted in whole numbers.

Continuous data

Information that can be expressed by any value within a given range. For example, the heights of pupils in a school are continuous data because the scale of measurement has a value at any point between the integers*. Temperature and time are also examples of continuous data.

Ordinal data

Information that can be placed in numerical order, for example, the height, age or income of 100 people.

Nominal data

Information that cannot be placed in numerical order, for example, the name, gender or place of birth of 100 people.

Primary data

Information that has been collected directly in a **survey**, investigation or experiment. For example, questioning a group of people, and recording daily temperatures over a period of time are ways of collecting primary data. Primary data that has not yet been organized or analyzed is called **raw data**.

Secondary data

Information that has already been collected and sorted, for example, information published by a market research company. Once **primary data** has been processed, it becomes secondary data.

Number of passengers	1	2	3	4
Number of cars	21	10	3	1

The table above shows the number of people in each car that passed a school's gates between 10am and 10:15am on one day. The data is secondary data: it has been sorted and you can easily draw conclusions, for example that most cars had only one person in.

Distribution (of a set of data)

Usually a table that shows how many there are of each type of data.

Number on die	1	2	3	4	5	6
Number of throws	11	8	13	9	8	11

A distribution of results when a die is thrown 60 times

Frequency

The number of times an event happens or a value occurs in a **distribution**. For example, in the distribution 12 9 11 12 5 12, the frequency of the number 12 is 3.

* **Data list** 99; **Integers** 6; **Length, Mass** 72; **Population, Sample** 98; **Speed** 73.

Collecting data

There are various methods of collecting information. The one you choose will depend on the subject you are researching. Whichever method you use, it is important to be aware how **bias** might be introduced, and plan how to reduce or avoid it.

Bias
An influence that might prevent results from fairly representing the truth. For example, if you asked 1,000 people from a town which football team was best, the answer might be biased toward their home-town team.

Observation
A method of collecting data by watching, counting or measuring and recording the results using a tape or video recorder, or by writing the information on an observation sheet. In **systematic observation**, the observer is not involved in the activity or event being observed. In **participant observation**, the observer is actively involved.

Survey
A method of collecting information from a sample* of a population* in order to draw conclusions about the whole population. Surveys often take the form of **interviews** or **questionnaires**.

Pilot survey
A **survey** carried out on a small number of people to find out if there are any problems with the questions or methods used, so improvements can be made before using the survey on a larger scale.

Census
An official count, for example, of the population, including information such as gender, age and job.

Interview
A method of collecting data by questioning people directly, either individually or in groups. In a **formal interview**, the questions follow a precise format. In an **informal interview**, the questions are more general, leading to a more loosely structured discussion about a subject.

Questionnaire
A set of questions on a form that is sent to a number of people in order to collect information on a specific subject. Questionnaires can be used to gather **qualitative data** or **quantitative data**. The best questions are simple, precise and unbiased (they should not lead toward any particular answer).

It is often helpful to limit the range of answers in some way. This makes it easier to analyze the information and make comparisons. For example, you could ask for an opinion in the following way:

School uniform should be compulsory.
Agree ☐   Disagree ☐   Undecided ☐

The questionnaire below forms part of a survey into the sales of a brand of ice cream. It provides basic information on the likes and dislikes of the people completing the questionnaire.

Dairy Frosty ice cream questionnaire

The following questions relate to your purchases of Dairy Frosty ice-cream Minicups in the past year. Please mark the appropriate box under each question.

1. Do you eat Dairy Frosty ice-cream Minicups?
   Yes ☐   No ☐

2. Which variety of Dairy Frosty ice-cream Minicups do you prefer?
   Strawberry ☐   Chocolate ☐   Vanilla ☐

3. Approximately how many Dairy Frosty ice-cream Minicups do you buy each month?
   1–5 ☐   6–10 ☐   11–15 ☐   More than15 ☐

4. How old are you?
   under 18 ☐   18–30 ☐   31–40 ☐
   41–50 ☐   51–60 ☐   over 60 ☐

5. A spoon should be supplied with each Minicup.
   Agree ☐   Disagree ☐   Undecided ☐

Thank you for taking the time to fill in this questionnaire. Please send it to Dairy Frosty in the pre-paid envelope provided.

Data logging
The method of using a computer to measure and record changes in conditions, such as the temperature of a room. Data is collected by sensors attached to the computer. These measure physical quantities such as temperature or light, and send the data to the computer, which uses **data logging software** to record the information in a **data log**. This software can also be used to analyze and display the data.

Sampling

A **sample** is a part of a whole set*. When conducting a survey*, it is often too expensive or too time consuming to interview every member of a set. In this situation, a sample can be taken. The sample should be representative of the whole group, and should not contain any bias*. Taking a sample is called **sampling**.

Population

The whole set from which a sample is taken. For example, if a sample of 100 boys aged 5–10 is taken, the population is all boys aged 5–10.

Convenience sampling

Taking a sample that is easy to collect, such as consulting friends or family.

Random sampling or simple random sampling

Selecting a sample in such a way that every member of a **population** has an equal chance of being chosen. There are many ways to do this, from picking names out of a hat to giving each member of the population a number and using a computer, calculator or chart to produce random numbers.

Random sampling is based on the idea that members of a population are **homogeneous** (the same). This is often not true, though, so the results from a small random sample are likely to be less accurate than those gathered from a larger group.

Systematic sampling

Using a particular system for choosing a sample. For example, a population might be placed in order of age and then every tenth person selected for the sample. A sample chosen by this method is less random than a **random sample**.

Quota sampling

Selecting a sample which contains a specified number of members of various groups within a **population**. These groups are selected before the sampling takes place. For example, a quota might include 50 men and 50 women, and require half of each group to wear glasses.

Stratified sampling

Making a selection by dividing a **population** into groups (called **strata**) according to certain characteristics, such as gender, and taking a **random** or **systematic sample** from each group. A stratified sample can better represent the population if the number chosen from each group for the sample is in the same proportion* as that group is to the population as a whole.

For example, to select a stratified sample of 50 pupils from three year groups containing 126, 105 and 119 people respectively, use:

$$\frac{\text{number from}}{\text{each stratum}} = \frac{\text{stratum}}{\text{population}} \times \text{total sample}$$

In this example, the population is the number of pupils in all three year groups.
Population = (126 + 105 + 119) = 350

$$\text{Year group 1} = \frac{126}{350} \times 50 = 18$$

$$\text{Year group 2} = \frac{105}{350} \times 50 = 15$$

$$\text{Year group 3} = \frac{119}{350} \times 50 = 17$$

So the stratified sample contains 18 pupils from year group 1, 15 from group 2 and 17 from group 3.

Multi-stage sampling

A method of selecting a sample from another sample. For example, if a sample of people aged over 50 were taken, a further sample of women aged over 50 could be taken from this group.

Cluster sampling

Dividing a **population** into groups called **clusters**, making a selection of clusters and including each member of the chosen clusters in the sample. For example, schools may each form a cluster, and each member of the selected school would be included in the sample.

Sampling error

The difference between the data gathered from a sample and the data for a whole **population**. For example, a local survey* of shoppers might show that a particular brand of cat food is most popular, but the sales figures for the whole state might show that another brand is more popular.

* **Average** 100; **Bar chart** 106; **Bias** 97; **Proportion** 23; **Set** 12; **Survey** 97.

Recording data

Data list

A method of recording data by writing down each item as it occurs (see illustration on page 96). Information in a data list needs sorting before any accurate conclusions can be drawn.

Tally chart

A method of recording data using one stroke, called a **tally**, to represent each item counted. Each group of five tallies is arranged 卌 (or ⬚), which makes it easier to count the groups.

Frequency table

A chart showing the number of times an event or value occurs (the frequency). A complete list of frequencies is called a **frequency distribution**.

*This frequency table shows sales of ice cream in one hour. The frequency distribution has been added to the **tally chart**.*

Ice cream	Tallies	Frequency
Vanilla	卌 ||	7
Chocolate	卌 |||	8
Strawberry	卌 卌	10

Cumulative frequency table

A chart showing the running total of the number of times an event or value occurs. This is called the **cumulative frequency**.

Length of journey (min)	Frequency	Cumulative frequency
1–10	7	7
11–20	8	7 + 8 = 15
21–30	10	15 + 10 = 25

The total cumulative frequency should equal the size of the sample.

Two-way table or contingency table

A table in which each row and column is associated with a particular category.

A two-way table showing the preferred sport of girls and boys in a class.

	Football	Swimming	Tennis
Boys	8	5	3
Girls	4	6	5

Computer database

A computer program that can store and sort large quantities of data. Many databases can also create diagrams, such as bar charts*, to illustrate the data, and calculate statistics such as averages*.

Grouping data

Grouped frequency distribution table

A chart showing the number of times a group of events or values occurs (the **grouped frequency**). A complete list of grouped frequencies is called a **grouped frequency distribution**.

Distance (miles)	Tallies	Frequency
under 5	卌		6
6–10	||	2
11–20	卌 ||||	9
21–30			1
over 30	||	2

*This table shows how far away from the office a group of workers live. From the grouped frequency distribution you can see that most people in the **sample** (9 out of 20) live between 11 and 20 miles away from the office.*

Class interval

A group or category in a **grouped frequency distribution table**. For example, the first class interval in the table above is "under 5." The lower and upper values of a class interval are called the **class limits**. For example, the **lower class limit** of the class interval 6–10 is 6, and the **upper class limit** is 10.

Class boundary

The border between two **class intervals**. To find the class boundary, add the **upper class limit** of one class interval to the **lower class limit** of the next class interval and divide by two. For example, the class boundary between the class intervals 11–20 and 21–30 is 20.5 (that is, (20 + 21) ÷ 2). The **lower class boundary** divides a class interval from the one below it. The **upper class boundary** divides a class interval from the one above it.

Class width, class length or class size

The difference between the **upper** and **lower class boundaries** of a **class interval**. For example, the class width of the class interval 21–30 is 10 (that is, 30.5 − 20.5).

Mid-interval value or midpoint

The middle value of a **class interval**. To find the mid-interval value, add the **lower** and **upper class limits** or **class boundaries** and divide by 2. For example, the mid-interval value of the class interval 11–20 is 15.5, calculated from the class limits (11 + 20) ÷ 2 or class boundaries (10.5 + 20.5) ÷ 2.

Internet links For links to useful websites on **gathering data**, go to *www.usborne-quicklinks.com*

AVERAGES

An **average** is a single value that is used to represent a collection of data*. Averages are sometimes called **measures of central tendency** or **measures of average**. Three commonly used types of averages are **mode**, **median** and **mean**.

Mode of a distribution

The value or values that occur most often in a distribution*. For example, the distribution of time in minutes taken by 10 people to finish a test is:

30   31   32   32   35   36   36   36   37   40

The value 36 occurs most often in this distribution, so the mode is 36.

Bimodal distribution

A distribution* that has two **modes**. For example, in the following distribution the values 32 and 36 both occur twice:

30   31   32   32   35   36   36   39

This means that 32 and 36 are both modes.

A distribution which has three or more modes is called a **multimodal distribution**.

Mode of a frequency distribution

To find the **mode** of a frequency distribution*, find the value with the highest frequency*.

Sock size	Frequency
Small	98
Medium	429
Large	342
Extra large	131

This table shows the frequency of the sizes of pairs of socks bought in a store in a month. You can see from the frequency table that the category with the highest frequency (429) is medium, so the mode of this distribution is medium.

Modal group or modal class

The class interval* of a grouped frequency distribution* that occurs most often.

Time (minutes)	Frequency
1–5	10
6–10	25
11–15	10
16–20	5

This table shows the length of time that 50 passengers had to wait for a bus one day. The modal group is 6–10 minutes as it has the highest frequency.

Median of a distribution

The middle value of a distribution* that is arranged in size order. To find the median position, use the formula*:
$$\text{median} = \tfrac{1}{2}(n + 1)$$
where n is the number of values.

For example, to find the median of the distribution:

4   3   1   8   5   2   1   6   12

1. Arrange the distribution in size order:

   1   1   2   3   4   5   6   8   12

2. Calculate the median position using:
   $$\text{median} = \tfrac{1}{2}(n + 1)$$
   $$= \tfrac{1}{2}(9 + 1) = \tfrac{1}{2} \times 10 = 5$$

3. Find the value that is in the median position, in this case, the 5th value in the list:

   1   1   2   3   4   5   6   8   12

The median of this distribution is 4.

If there is an even number of values, the median position is halfway between two middle values.

1   1   2   3   4   5   5   6   8   12

To find the median, add the middle values and divide by two:
$$\text{median} = \frac{4 + 5}{2} = 4.5$$
The median of this distribution is 4.5.

Median of a frequency distribution

To find the **median** of a frequency distribution*, first calculate the cumulative frequency* of the distribution. Calculate the median position and find the value that is in that position.

If the median position is 0.5 more than a cumulative frequency, add together the corresponding value and the value above it and divide by two. In the example below, the median position is 25.5 (that is, (50 + 1) ÷ 2). This is 0.5 above the cumulative frequency 25, so the median value is 7.5 (that is, (7 + 8) ÷ 2).

Value	Frequency	Cumulative frequency
6	12	12
7	13	12 + 13 = 25
8	14	25 + 14 = 39
9	11	39 + 11 = 50

Median of a grouped frequency distribution

To find the **median** of a grouped frequency distribution*, read the value at the median position on a cumulative frequency diagram (see page 109).

* **Class interval** 99; **Continuous data** 96; **Cumulative frequency (table)** 99; **Data, Discrete data, Distribution** 96; **Formula** 75; **Frequency** 96; **Frequency distribution** 99 (**Frequency table**); **Grouped frequency distribution (table)** 99; **Mid-interval value** 99; **Product** 14 (**Multiplication**); **Sum** 14 (**Addition**)

Mean or **arithmetic mean of a distribution**

A measure of the general size of the data. To find the mean, use the rule:

$$\text{mean} = \frac{\Sigma \text{ values}}{\text{number of values}}$$

where the Greek letter sigma, Σ, means "the total of" or "the sum* of."

For example, to find the mean of the distribution*:

$$0 \quad 5 \quad 7 \quad 6 \quad 2 \quad 10$$

use

$$\frac{(0 + 5 + 7 + 6 + 2 + 10)}{6} = \frac{30}{6} = 5$$

The mean of this distribution is 5.

The rule for finding the mean can also be written as:

$$\bar{x} = \frac{\Sigma x}{n}$$

where $\bar{x}$ is the mean, x is the set of values and n is the number of values in the set.

Mean of a frequency distribution

To find the **mean** of a frequency distribution*, first find the sum* of the values by multiplying each value (x) by its frequency* (f) and adding these products*. Then find the mean using:

$$\text{mean} = \frac{\Sigma \text{ values}}{\text{number of values}}$$

For example, the frequency distribution table below shows the number of books read by a group of students in one month. To find the mean of this distribution, first find the sum of the values, as described above.

Number of books (x)	Frequency (f)	Frequency × value (fx)
0	1	$1 \times 0 = 0$
1	2	$2 \times 1 = 2$
2	0	$0 \times 2 = 0$
3	1	$1 \times 3 = 3$
4	1	$1 \times 4 = 4$
5	2	$2 \times 5 = 10$
6	0	$0 \times 6 = 0$
7	1	$1 \times 7 = 7$
	$\Sigma f = 8$	$\Sigma fx = 26$

Then calculate the mean using:

$$\text{mean} = \frac{\Sigma \text{ values}}{\text{number of values}} = \frac{26}{8} = 3.25$$

The mean of this frequency distribution is 3.25 books. A mean value does not have to be a whole number, even when the data is discrete*.

Mean of a grouped frequency distribution

To find the **mean** of a grouped frequency distribution*, find the mid-interval value* (x) for each class interval* and multiply it by the frequency* (f). Then add the products* to find the total sum* of the values and find the mean using:

$$\text{mean} = \frac{\Sigma \text{ values}}{\text{number of values}}$$

This method can be used for finding the mean of discrete* and continuous data*. As the exact values in a grouped frequency distribution are not known, the mean is calculated using the mid-interval value, which is itself an average. For this reason, the mean of a grouped frequency distribution can be only an approximation.

For example, the grouped frequency distribution table* below shows how many points were scored by 60 contestants in a general knowledge quiz.

Points scored	Mid-interval value (x)	Frequency (f)	Mid-interval value × frequency (fx)
0–10	5.0	1	$5.0 \times 1 = 5.0$
11–20	15.5	2	$15.5 \times 2 = 31$
21–30	25.5	4	$25.5 \times 4 = 102$
31–40	35.5	3	$35.5 \times 3 = 106.5$
41–50	45.5	9	$45.5 \times 9 = 409.5$
51–60	55.5	14	$55.5 \times 14 = 777$
61–70	65.5	12	$65.5 \times 12 = 786$
71–80	75.5	9	$75.5 \times 9 = 679.5$
81–90	85.5	5	$85.5 \times 5 = 427.5$
91–100	95.5	1	$95.5 \times 1 = 95.5$
		$\Sigma f = 60$	$\Sigma fx = 3419.5$

To calculate an estimate of the mean number of points scored in the quiz, use:

$$\text{mean} = \frac{\Sigma \text{ values}}{\text{number of values}}$$

$$= \frac{3,419.5}{60}$$

$$= 56.99 \ (2 \text{ d.p.})$$

The mean number of points scored in the quiz was approximately 57.

Internet links For links to useful websites on **averages**, go to www.usborne-quicklinks.com

MEASURES OF SPREAD

Spread, or **dispersion**, is a measure of how much a collection of data* is spread out. There are several methods of describing dispersion. These are known as **measures of dispersion** and they give different types of information about the spread of the data.

Range

The **range** of a distribution* is the difference between the highest and lowest values. (This must be a single value.) To find the range of a distribution, use the rule:

range = highest value − lowest value

For example, to find the range of this distribution, take the lowest value from the highest:

$$2 \quad 10 \quad 3 \quad 7 \quad 11 \quad 5 \quad 3 \quad 9 \quad 6$$
$$\text{range} = 11 - 2 = 9$$

To find the range of a grouped frequency distribution*, take the lowest possible value from the highest possible value. For example, if the first group were 0–5 and the last group were 46–50, the range would be 50 (50 − 0).

Comparing distributions

To learn more about a set of distributions, it can be helpful to compare the range and the mean*. For example, this table shows the ages of residents in two nursing homes:

	Age							Total
Bluebells	67	72	99	69	81	63	102	553
The Elms	77	78	82	79	78	80	79	553

The mean age at each home is 79 (that is, 553 ÷ 7). The range of ages at Bluebells is 35 years (102 − 67) and the range of ages at The Elms is 5 years (82 − 77). This shows that, although the mean age is the same, the range of ages at Bluebells is much greater.

Quartiles

Lower quartile or **first quartile** (Q_1)
The value that lies one quarter of the way through a distribution* arranged in ascending order. To find the lower quartile position, use:

$$\text{lower quartile position} = \frac{(n+1)}{4}$$

where n is the number of values in the distribution, or the cumulative frequency* of a frequency distribution* or grouped frequency distribution*.

Upper quartile or **third quartile** (Q_3)
The value that lies three-quarters of the way through a distribution* arranged in ascending order. To find the upper quartile position, use:

$$\text{upper quartile position} = \frac{3(n+1)}{4}$$

where n is the number of values in the distribution, or the cumulative frequency* of a frequency distribution* or grouped frequency distribution*.

To find the quartiles of a distribution if the quartile position is a decimal*, or to find the quartiles of a frequency distribution or a grouped frequency distribution, draw a cumulative frequency diagram* and read off the values at the quartile positions.

Interquartile range (IQR)
The range of the middle 50% of a distribution*, which eliminates extreme values at either end of the distribution. To find the interquartile range, use:

IQR = upper quartile − lower quartile

For example, to find the interquartile range of:

$$2 \quad 4 \quad 5 \quad 7 \quad 7 \quad 9 \quad 12 \quad 15 \quad 16 \quad 16 \quad 18$$

1. Find the value in the **lower quartile** position:
$$\frac{n+1}{4} = \frac{11+1}{4} = \frac{12}{4} = 3$$
The 3rd value in the distribution is 5, so the lower quartile is 5.

2. Find the value in the **upper quartile** position:
$$\frac{3(n+1)}{4} = \frac{3 \times (11+1)}{4} = \frac{36}{4} = 9$$
The 9th value in the distribution is 16, so the upper quartile is 16.

3. Take the lower quartile value from the upper quartile value (16 − 5 = 11). The interquartile range of this distribution is 11.

* **Cumulative frequency diagram** 109; **Cumulative frequency table** 99; **Data** 96; **Decimal** 19; **Distribution** 96; **Formula** 75; **Frequency distribution** 99 (**Frequency table**); **Grouped frequency distribution** (**table**) 99; **Mean** 100; **Substitution** 77; **Sum** 14 (**Addition**).

Standard deviation

Standard deviation from the mean*, usually known as **standard deviation**, tells you how spread out the values in a distribution* are from its mean. Unlike **range** and **interquartile range**, standard deviation takes into account every value of a distribution. A high standard deviation means that the values are very spread out, while a low standard deviation means that the values are close together. Standard deviation is given in the same units as the original data. It is represented by the lower-case Greek letter sigma, σ.

Standard deviation calculation method 1

$$\text{standard deviation } (\sigma) = \sqrt{\frac{\Sigma(x - \bar{x})^2}{n}}$$

where x is each value in the distribution, $\bar{x}$ is the mean of the distribution, n is the total number of values and Σ means "the total of" or "the sum* of."

For example, the distribution below shows the number of years for which eight employees have worked for a company:

$$1 \quad 5 \quad 6 \quad 3 \quad 2 \quad 10 \quad 7 \quad 6$$

To find the standard deviation:

1. Calculate the mean ($\bar{x}$) of the distribution:

$$\text{mean} = \frac{\Sigma \text{ values}}{\text{number of values}}$$

$$= \frac{(1 + 5 + 6 + 3 + 2 + 10 + 7 + 6)}{8}$$

$$= \frac{40}{8} = 5$$

2. Find the difference between each value in the distribution and the mean ($x - \bar{x}$):

$$^-4 \quad 0 \quad 1 \quad ^-2 \quad ^-3 \quad 5 \quad 2 \quad 1$$

3. Find the square of each of these values ($x - \bar{x}$)^2:

$$16 \quad 0 \quad 1 \quad 4 \quad 9 \quad 25 \quad 4 \quad 1$$

4. Find the mean of the squares of the differences, known as the **variance** $\left(\frac{\Sigma(x - \bar{x})^2}{n}\right)$:

$$\frac{16 + 0 + 1 + 4 + 9 + 25 + 4 + 1}{8}$$

$$= \frac{60}{8} = 7.5$$

5. Find the square root of the variance $\left(\sqrt{\frac{\Sigma(x - \bar{x})^2}{n}}\right)$

$\sqrt{7.5} = 2.74$ (3 s.f.)

The standard deviation is 2.74 years (to 3 s.f.).

Standard deviation calculation method 2

$$\text{standard deviation } (\sigma) = \sqrt{\frac{\Sigma x^2}{n} - \left(\frac{\Sigma x}{n}\right)^2}$$

where x is each value in the distribution*, n is the total number of values and Σ means "the total of" or "the sum* of."

For example, the distribution below shows the number of years for which eight employees have worked for a company:

$$1 \quad 5 \quad 6 \quad 3 \quad 2 \quad 10 \quad 7 \quad 6$$

To find the standard deviation:

1. Place the values in a table and calculate the value of x^2 for each value of x.

x	x^2
1	1
5	25
6	36
3	9
2	4
10	100
7	49
6	36
$\Sigma x = 40$	$\Sigma x^2 = 260$

2. Find the mean of the squares of the distribution:

$$\frac{\Sigma x^2}{n} = \frac{260}{8} = 32.5$$

3. Calculate the mean of the distribution and square it:

$$\left(\frac{\Sigma x}{n}\right)^2 = \left(\frac{40}{8}\right)^2 = 5^2 = 25$$

4. Find the standard deviation by substituting* the values into the formula*:

$$\sigma = \sqrt{\frac{\Sigma x^2}{n} - \left(\frac{\Sigma x}{n}\right)^2}$$

$$= \sqrt{32.5 - 25} = \sqrt{7.5} = 2.74 \text{ (3 s.f.)}$$

The standard deviation is 2.74 years (to 3 s.f.).

Variance

The square of the **standard deviation**. The variance is expressed by the formula*:

$$\frac{\Sigma(x - \bar{x})^2}{n} \quad \text{or} \quad \frac{\Sigma x^2}{n} - \left(\frac{\Sigma x}{n}\right)^2$$

where x is each value in the distribution*, $\bar{x}$ is the mean of the distribution, n is the total number of values and Σ means "the total of" or "the sum* of."

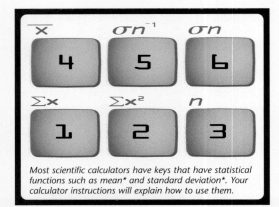

Most scientific calculators have keys that have statistical functions such as mean* and standard deviation*. Your calculator instructions will explain how to use them.

To find the standard deviation of a grouped frequency distribution

Take the mid-interval value* of each class interval* as the x value and use either of the methods of finding standard deviation* described on page 103. The standard deviation formulas* need to be altered to take into account the fact that each value has to be multiplied by the frequency* (f).

For example, the grouped frequency distribution table* below shows the number of telephone calls received on one day by workers in an office. To find an estimate for the standard deviation:

1. Calculate values for x and, as it is a grouped frequency distribution, find fx and fx².

Calls	f	x	fx	fx²
1–5	9	3	27	$27 \times 3 = 81$
6–10	15	8	120	$120 \times 8 = 960$
11–15	13	13	169	$169 \times 13 = 2{,}197$
16–20	3	18	54	$54 \times 18 = 972$
	$\Sigma f = 40$		$\Sigma fx = 370$	$\Sigma fx^2 = 4{,}210$

2. Find the mean* of the squares* of the grouped frequency distribution:

$$\frac{\Sigma fx^2}{n} = \frac{4210}{40} = 105.25$$

3. Find the mean of the grouped frequency distribution and square it:

$$\left(\frac{\Sigma fx}{n}\right)^2 = \left(\frac{370}{40}\right)^2 = 9.25^2 = 85.5625$$

4. Find the standard deviation by substituting* the values into the formula:

$$\sigma = \sqrt{\frac{\Sigma fx^2}{n} - \left(\Sigma fx \backslash n\right)^2} = \sqrt{105.25 - 85.5625}$$

$$= \sqrt{19.6875} = 4.44 \text{ (3 s.f.)}$$

The standard deviation is approximately 4.44 calls (to 3 s.f.).

Changes in standard deviation

If every value in a distribution* is increased (or decreased) by the same amount, the mean* is increased (or decreased) by that amount, but the standard deviation stays the same.

For example, the distribution below has a mean of 6 and a standard deviation of 2.83 (3 s.f.):

$$2 \quad 4 \quad 6 \quad 8 \quad 10$$

If every value is decreased by 3 to give:

$$^-1 \quad 1 \quad 3 \quad 5 \quad 7$$

The new mean is calculated as:

$$\frac{(^-1 + 1 + 3 + 5 + 7)}{5} = \frac{15}{5} = 3$$

The new standard deviation is calculated as:

$$\sqrt{\frac{(1 + 1 + 9 + 25 + 49)}{5} - \left(\frac{15}{5}\right)^2}$$

$$= \sqrt{\frac{85}{5} - \left(\frac{15}{5}\right)^2}$$

$$= \sqrt{17 - 9} = \sqrt{8} = 2.83 \text{ (3 s.f.)}$$

The mean of the new distribution is increased by 3 (3 + 3 = 6), but the standard deviation is the same for both distributions (2.83).

If every value in a distribution is multiplied (or divided) by the same number, the standard deviation and the mean will both be multiplied (or divided) by that amount.

For example, if every value of the original distribution above is multiplied by 2, to give:

$$4 \quad 8 \quad 12 \quad 16 \quad 20$$

The new mean is calculated as:

$$\frac{(4 + 8 + 12 + 16 + 20)}{5}$$

$$= \frac{60}{5} = 12$$

The new standard deviation is calculated as:

$$\sqrt{\frac{(16 + 64 + 144 + 256 + 400)}{5} - \left(\frac{60}{5}\right)^2}$$

$$= \sqrt{\frac{880}{5} - 12^2}$$

$$= \sqrt{176 - 144} = \sqrt{32} = 5.66 \text{ (3 s.f.)}$$

The mean of the new distribution is twice that of the original distribution (that is, $6 \times 2 = 12$) and the standard deviation is also doubled (that is, $2.83 \times 2 = 5.66$).

* **Angle** 32; **Area** 55; **Class interval** 99; **Data, Distribution** 96; **Formula** 75; **Frequency** 96; **Frequency table** 99; **Grouped frequency distribution** (table) 99; **Mean** 101; **Mid-interval value** 99; **Protractor** 47; **Rounding** 16; **Sector** 65; **Squaring** 8 (**Square numbers**); **Standard deviation** 103; **Substitution** 77; **Sum** 14 (**Addition**).

REPRESENTING DATA

There are many different types of diagrams and charts you can use to illustrate data*. The methods you choose might depend on what you would like to show, as some methods emphasize slightly different aspects of the information.

Pictogram, pictograph or ideograph

A chart on which pictures are used to show the frequency* of a distribution*. A pictogram includes a title and a key, explaining what the pictures mean. Part of a picture can be used to represent smaller quantities.

Number of ice cream cones sold in a week

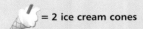

Monday	🍦🍦
Tuesday	🍦🍦🍦
Wednesday	🍦🍦
Thursday	🍦
Friday	🍦🍦🍦
Saturday	🍦🍦🍦🍦
Sunday	🍦🍦🍦

🍦 = 2 ice cream cones

If different symbols are used, they should be the same width as each other and aligned on the chart. It is also helpful if each symbol represents the same number of items. This avoids giving a misleading impression of the results.

= 2 ice cream cones

= 2 ice pops

= 2 hot dogs

These pictures are the same size and represent the same number of items.

Pie chart

A diagram in which the frequency* of a distribution* is represented by the angles* (or areas*) of the sectors* of a circle. The title of the pie chart tells you what it is showing, and labels or a key explain what each sector represents.

How a company's employees usually travel to work

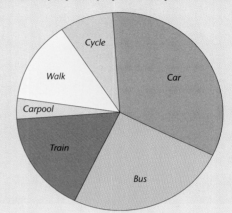

To find the size of the angle that will represent each frequency, use the formula*:

$$\text{angle} = f \times \frac{360°}{\Sigma f}$$

where f is the frequency.

For example, the frequency table* below shows the data that was used to create the pie chart above. In this example, $\Sigma f = 60$, so

$$\text{angle} = f \times \frac{360°}{60} = f \times 6°$$

Transport	Frequency	Angle
Car	20	20 × 6° = 120°
Bus	15	15 × 6° = 90°
Train	10	10 × 6° = 60°
Carpool	2	2 × 6° = 12°
Walk	8	8 × 6° = 48°
Cycle	5	5 × 6° = 30°
	$\Sigma f = 60$	Σ angles = 360°

The sum* of the angles must always be 360°. It is sometimes necessary to round* the angles to the nearest degree. If so, for every angle you round up, you will need to round another one down. Use a protractor* to measure the angles at the center of your pie chart.

Bar chart

A chart that uses vertical* or horizontal* bars of equal width to show the frequency* of a distribution*. The title tells you what the bar chart shows, and labels on the axes* explain what they represent and, where appropriate, give the units that are used. A bar chart showing discrete data* has gaps between the bars, but one showing continuous data* has no gaps.

Favorite drinks of 100 people

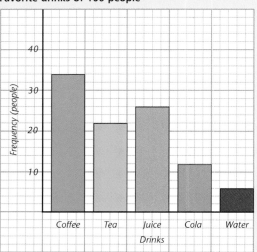

Compound bar chart or multiple bar chart

A **bar chart** that uses multiple bars within a category to illustrate more than one set of data.

Favorite drinks of 100 people

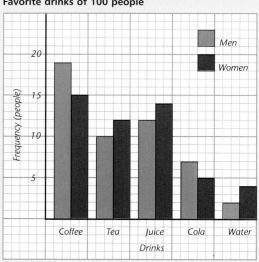

Component bar chart, composite bar chart, sectional bar chart or stacked bar chart

A **bar chart** that divides each bar into sections to illustrate more than one set of data.

For example, the component bar chart below uses the same data as the **compound bar chart** opposite, with the bar representing each gender being subdivided to show their preferred drink.

Favorite drinks of 100 people

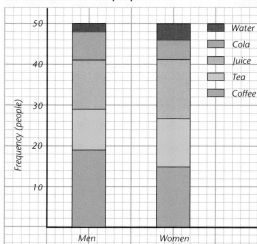

The component bar chart below shows the same information but this time with the bar representing each drink being subdivided to show the split between genders.

Favorite drinks of 100 people

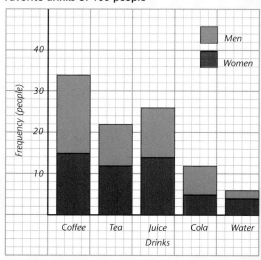

* **Area** 55; **Axes** 31 (**Cartesian coordinate system**); **Class boundary, Class interval, Class width** 99; **Continuous data, Discrete data, Distribution, Frequency** 96; **Grouped frequency distribution** (**table**) 99; **Horizontal** 30; **Polygon** 34; **Proportional** 25; **Sum** 14 (**Addition**); **Vertical** 30.

Histogram

A **bar chart** in which the area* of each bar is proportional* to the frequency* of a grouped frequency distribution*. The bars of a histogram are drawn at the class boundaries*. The height of each bar is called the **frequency density**.

To plot a histogram from a grouped frequency distribution, first find the class width* for each class interval*, then calculate the frequency density, using the rule:

$$\text{frequency density} = \frac{\text{frequency}}{\text{class width}}$$

For example, the grouped frequency distribution table* below shows the time taken by 25 people to finish a newspaper crossword. Time is continuous data* so it is measured to the nearest minute. The 1–5 class interval therefore extends from 0.5–5.5 minutes, so its class width is 5. The other class widths are calculated in the same way.

Time (minutes)	Frequency	Class width	Frequency density
1–4	1	4	1 ÷ 4 = 0.25
4–6	5	2	5 ÷ 2 = 2.5
7–8	9	2	9 ÷ 2 = 4.5
9–16	6	8	6 ÷ 8 = 0.75
17–20	4	4	4 ÷ 4 = 1

Draw the histogram, plotting the frequency density against the class intervals. Label the axes* and give the histogram a title.

Time taken to finish crossword

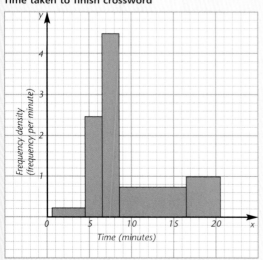

Time (minutes)

To calculate frequency from a histogram

Use the rule below, which is the rearranged rule for calculating frequency density:

frequency = class width × frequency density

This is the same as finding the area* of each of the bars. So, to find the total frequency of people who finished the crossword:

frequency = (4 × 0.25) + (2 × 2.5) + (2 × 4.5) +
$\qquad$ (8 × 0.75) + (4 × 1)
$\qquad$ = 1 + 5 + 9 + 6 + 4
$\qquad$ = 25

The total frequency should be the sum* of the frequencies in the table.

Frequency polygon

A chart on which the frequency* (or **frequency density**) is plotted against the mid-interval values* of class intervals*. The points are joined by a series of straight lines and extended to the horizontal* axis* to form a polygon*.

A frequency polygon can also be drawn on a **bar chart** or **histogram**, by joining the midpoints of the tops of the bars. The area* under the polygon is equal to the area under the histogram.

For example, the frequency polygon below is drawn from the histogram illustrating the time taken to finish a crossword (see left).

Time taken to finish crossword

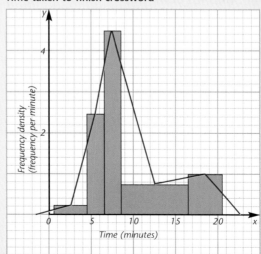

Time (minutes)

Stem-and-leaf display or stem-and-leaf diagram

A method of representing data* by splitting the numbers of the distribution* into two parts. It is most often used to show the range* and spread* of small amounts of quantitative data*.

For example, to arrange the distribution below in a stem-and-leaf display, write the tens in the "stem" column, in ascending order, and then write the units in the "leaf" column.

| 13 | 10 | 14 | 12 | 14 | 9 | 23 | 13 | 13 | 21 |

Stem	Leaves
0	9
1	0 2 3 3 3 4 4
2	1 3

Key: 2|3 stands for 23

The leaves are usually arranged in ascending order too, especially if the display is to be used to find more information, such as the mode*, median* or range. Turned on its side, the pattern of the leaves is like a bar chart*, but it has the advantage of showing individual values within the distribution.

The leaves column can only include one digit from each number, but the stem can contain any number of digits. For example, the stem-and-leaf display below represents the distribution:

| 205 | 216 | 233 | 239 | 240 | 240 | 248 |

Stem	Leaves
20	5
21	6
22	
23	3 9
24	0 0 8

Key: 24|8 stands for 248

To find the median value of the distribution, count the leaves from either end of the diagram until you reach the median position. For example, the display above has 7 leaves so 4 is the median position (7 + 1 ÷ 2). The 4th value is 9, so 239 is the median.

To find the mode, look for the number that occurs most frequently. In this case, the mode is 240.

The range is 248 − 205, which is 43.

Stem-and-leaf display with large sets of data

To display a larger distribution as a stem-and-leaf diagram, the stem can be subdivided into upper and lower parts to make it easier to read. For example, the stem-and-leaf display below includes a large amount of data* with a small range* so it looks very crowded:

Stem	Leaves
0	1 1 2 3 3 4 5 6 6 7 8
1	1 1 2 3 4 6 8 9
2	0 2 2 6

Key: 2|6 stands for 26

By using a − sign to represent the lower part of the stem (0–4) and a + sign to represent the upper part (5–9), the diagram becomes easier to read.

Stem	Leaves
0−	1 1 2 3 3 4
0+	5 6 6 7 8
1−	1 1 2 3 4
1+	6 8 9
2−	0 2 2
2+	6

Key: 2+|6 stands for 26

Back to back stem-and-leaf display

A stem-and-leaf display that shows two sets of data. To construct a back to back stem-and-leaf display, first choose appropriate units to build the stem. Then form the leaves by writing the remaining digits of one data set to the left of the stem, and those of the other data set to the right. For example, to represent the two distributions from the table below in a stem-and-leaf display:

A	19	20	23	23	27	30	30
B	8	17	21	27	31	31	40

1. Build the stem of the diagram, including the tens digits from both sets of data.
2. Form the leaves by writing the units of each set on either side of the stem:

Data A		Data B
	0	8
9	1	7
7 3 3 0	2	1 7
0 0	3	1 1
	4	0

Key: 0 | 3 | 1 stands for 30 and 31

*Bar chart 106; Cumulative frequency 99; Data, Distribution 96; Graph (algebraic) 80; Grouped frequency distribution table 99; Interquartile range, Lower quartile 102; Median, Mode 100; Quantitative data 96; Random sample 98; Range, Spread 102; Upper class boundary 99 (Class boundary); Upper quartile 102; Vertical 30.

Cumulative frequency diagram

A graph* on which the cumulative frequencies* of a distribution* are plotted and the points are joined. On a **cumulative frequency curve**, the points are joined by a smooth curve, as shown in the example below. This type of diagram is also sometimes called an **ogive**, although the term is becoming less common. If the points are joined by a straight line, the diagram is a **cumulative frequency polygon**.

For example, the grouped frequency distribution table* below shows the length of time (to the nearest minute) that a random sample* of customers had to wait in a queue.

Time (minutes)	Frequency	Cumulative frequency
0–2	5	5
3–5	8	5 + 8 = 13
6–8	20	13 + 20 = 33
9–11	11	33 + 11 = 44
12–14	6	44 + 6 = 50
15–17	4	50 + 4 = 54
18–20	1	54 + 1 = 55

The cumulative frequency diagram is drawn by plotting the cumulative frequencies against the upper class boundaries*. The line or curve on both types of cumulative frequency diagram starts at zero on the cumulative frequency axis.

Time spent waiting in a queue

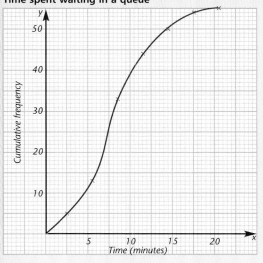

Using cumulative frequency diagrams

Cumulative frequency diagrams can be used to find out further information about the data*. For example, to find the number of people who waited 10 minutes or less, find the point at 10 minutes on the x-axis, and draw a vertical* line up to the graph*. Look on the y-axis to find the cumulative frequency* at this point. Where $x = 10$, $y = 39$ (approximately), so 39 people waited 10 minutes or less. 16 people waited more than 10 minutes (total number of people (55) − 39).

To find the median* waiting time, first find the median position. If the total cumulative frequency is greater than or equal to 100, use $\frac{n+1}{2}$. If, as in this case, it is less then 100, use $\frac{1}{2}(n + 1)$:

$$\frac{1}{2}(55 + 1) = \frac{1}{2} \times 56 = 28$$

Where $y = 28$, $x = 7.75$ (approximately), so the median waiting time is about 7.75 minutes.

To find the interquartile range*, subtract the lower quartile* from the upper quartile*.

$$\text{Upper quartile position} = \frac{3(n + 1)}{4} = \frac{3(55 + 1)}{4} = 42$$

Where $y = 42$, $x = 11$ (approximately), so the upper quartile is 11.

$$\text{Lower quartile position} = \frac{n + 1}{4} = \frac{55 + 1}{4} = 14$$

Where $y = 14$, $x = 5.75$ (approximately), so the lower quartile is 5.75. The interquartile range is 5.25 minutes (11 − 5.75).

Time spent waiting in a queue

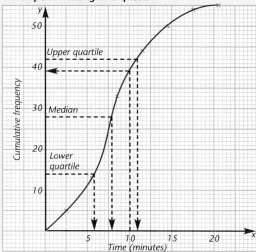

Five number summary

The lowest value, lower quartile*, median*, upper quartile* and highest value of a distribution*. These values enable you to assess the range* and interquartile range* of the data* and see how symmetrically* spread it is around the median.

Box plot or box-and-whisker diagram

A diagram that shows the **five number summary** of a distribution*. Box plots can be a useful way of comparing the spreads* of two or more distributions on the same number line*.

Each diagram contains a rectangular **box**. Its length represents the interquartile range*, but it can be any height as this is not significant. A vertical* line divides the box at the median*. At each end of the box, lines called **whiskers** extend horizontally* to the lowest and highest values to show the range* of the distribution.

For example, the box plot below illustrates the following distributions:

| Sample A | 3 | 10 | 10 | 12 | 12 | 13 | 15 | 20 |
| Sample B | 6 | 8 | 9 | 11 | 11 | 12 | 14 | 16 |

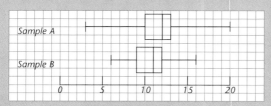

A variation on a box plot includes points to represent each piece of data, so not losing any of the detail.

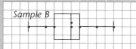

Sometimes the data* includes a value that is much higher or lower than all the rest, perhaps because of an error in measuring. These values, called **outliers**, are represented by an individual point or asterisk (*) beyond the whisker.

Zig-zag

A ripple in an axis* indicating that the scale does not apply to that section of the axis.

Line graph

A graph on which frequencies* of a distribution* are plotted, and the points are joined by a series of straight lines. The title tells you what the line graph shows. The labels on the axes* explain what they represent and, where appropriate, give the units that are used.

Average maximum temperature in Hamburg, Germany

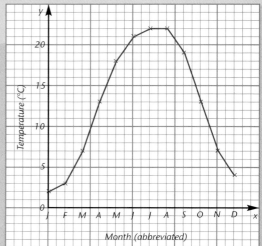

Month (abbreviated)

Scatter graph or scatter diagram

A graph on which points are plotted to show the relationship between two sets of quantitative data*. The points are not joined, and you can have several points with the same x or y value. The title and axis* labels tell you what the graph shows.

Marks achieved by pupils in French and German test

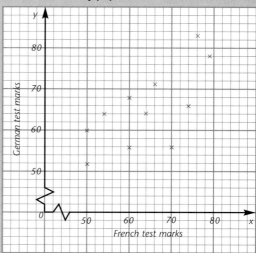

French test marks

* **Axes** 31 (**Cartesian coordinate system**); **Data, Distribution** 96; **Frequency** 96; **Horizontal** 30; **Interquartile range** 102; **Lower quartile** 102; **Mean** 101; **Median** 100; **Number line** 7 (**Directed numbers**); **Quantitative data** 96; **Range, Spread** 102; **Symmetrical** 42 (**Introduction**); **Upper quartile** 102; **Vertical** 30.

Correlation

A relationship between two sets of values. A **scatter graph** can show whether there is any correlation between the sets of data* it represents. An upward trend in the position of points on a scatter graph is called **positive correlation**. A downward trend is called **negative correlation**.

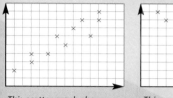

This scatter graph shows a positive correlation.

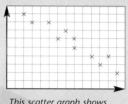

This scatter graph shows a negative correlation.

A scatter graph with points that lie on, or close to, a straight line has a **strong correlation**.

A strong correlation indicates that the two sets of values are closely related to each other.

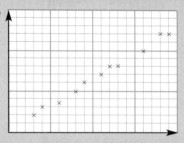

A scatter graph with points lying roughly in a straight line has a **moderate correlation**.

A moderate correlation indicates that the two sets of values are often related to each other.

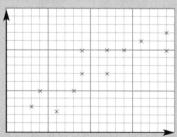

A scatter graph on which the points seem unrelated to a straight line is said to have **no correlation**.

No correlation indicates that the two sets of values are not related in any linear way, although other relationships might exist between them.

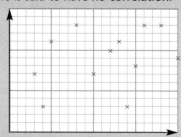

Line of best fit or regression line

A line drawn on a **scatter graph** to show the **correlation** between the two sets of values. Often, the line can be drawn by eye. However, to draw a more accurate line, find the mean* of each distribution* and draw a line at right angles (90°) to the axis* at this point. Then draw the line of best fit through the point where the two lines from the means meet.

For example, the table below shows the number of swimming pool lengths swum in various times.

Time (mins)	5	8	10	13	15	18	20	23
Lengths	11	15	23	27	31	40	39	50

To show the correlation between these values, plot them on a **scatter graph**, then draw a line of best fit through the point that represents the mean of both sets of data (shown on the graph by the symbol ⊗).

The mean length of time is:

$$\frac{5 + 8 + 10 + 13 + 15 + 18 + 20 + 23}{8} = \frac{112}{8} = 14$$

The mean number of lengths is:

$$= \frac{11 + 15 + 23 + 27 + 31 + 40 + 39 + 50}{8}$$

$$= \frac{236}{8} = 29.5$$

So, the line of best fit should be drawn through the point (14, 29.5). In this case, the line starts at (0,0) (as in no time, no lengths would be swum).

Number of lengths swum

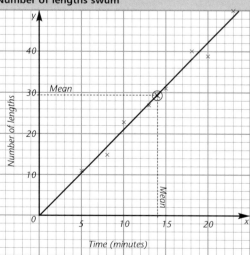

PROBABILITY

Probability is a branch of statistics* that allows you to calculate how likely something is to happen, and give this likelihood a numerical value. For example, if you toss a coin, there are two possible results: either it will land showing the head or the tail. The likelihood of it showing the head is 1 of the 2 results. This probability can be expressed as a fraction* ($\frac{1}{2}$), a decimal* (0.5), or a percentage* (50%).

Event

Something that happens, for example, the tossing of a coin or the throwing of a pair of dice.

Outcome

The result of an **event**, for example, a tossed coin landing heads up or a thrown die showing a six.

Success

The required result. For example, if you want a coin to land heads up and it does, this would be a **successful outcome**.

Equiprobable events

Events with equally likely **outcomes**. For example, if you toss a coin, there is an equal chance of the outcome being a head or a tail.

Probability scale

A scale measuring the likelihood of an **outcome**. The probability of an outcome that will certainly happen is 1. For example, the probability that you will be a little older by the time you have read this sentence is 1. An outcome with a probability of 1 is described as a **certainty**. The probability of an outcome that will certainly not happen is 0. For example, the probability that you will turn into an elephant is 0. An outcome with a probability of 0 is described as an **impossibility**.

The values 0 and 1 are the **extremes of probability**, and the probability of an outcome occurring can be anywhere between or including 0 and 1. The closer a probability is to 0 on the scale, the less likely the outcome is. The closer a probability is to 1, the more likely the outcome.

Theoretical probability

The probability of an **outcome** occurring in theory. Theoretical probability is based on equally likely outcomes: that is, no bias or error is involved.

The rule for calculating theoretical probability is:

$$P(\text{success}) = \frac{\text{total successful outcomes}}{\text{total possible outcomes}}$$

where P stands for "the probability of."

For example, if a bag contains 6 red balls and 4 blue balls, the theoretical probability of choosing a blue ball at random is:

$$P(\text{choosing a blue ball}) = \frac{4}{10} = \frac{2}{5}$$

The theoretical probability of choosing a blue ball at random is $\frac{2}{5}$. This could also be written as a decimal, 0.4, or as a percentage, 40%.

Experimental probability or relative frequency

The number of times an **outcome** occurs in an experiment.

The rule for calculating experimental probability is:

$$P(\text{success}) = \frac{\text{total successful outcomes}}{\text{total events}}$$

where P stands for "the probability of."

For example, if a die is thrown 100 times and it lands on 6 a total of 12 times, the experimental probability, or relative frequency, of throwing the die and getting a 6 is:

$$P(\text{throwing a six}) = \frac{12}{100} = \frac{3}{25}$$

The experimental probability of throwing the die and getting a 6 is $\frac{3}{25}$. This could also be written as a decimal, 0.12, or as a percentage, 12%.

* **Decimal** 19; **Fraction** 17; **Percentage** 27; **Statistics** 96 (**Data**).

Types of events

Single event
An **event** that involves only one item, for example tossing one coin.

Compound event or multiple event
An **event** that involves more than one item, for example, tossing two coins, or tossing a coin and a die.

Independent event
An **event** that has an **outcome** which is not affected by any other event. An independent event is also called a **random event**.

For example, when a die is thrown twice, the chance of throwing a particular number on the second occasion is not affected by the first event. The probability of getting a 6 is the same no matter how many times the die is thrown.

Dependent event
An **event** that has an **outcome** which is affected by another event.

For example, if a marble is taken at random from a bag of blue and green marbles, and is not put back into the bag, the color of the second marble to be picked will be dependent on the first event.

If there are 3 blue marbles and 3 green marbles:

P (choosing a blue marble) $= \frac{3}{6} = \frac{1}{2}$

If a blue marble is taken out and not replaced, the probability of picking another blue marble is now $\frac{2}{5}$ (as there are only 2 blue marbles and 5 marbles altogether).

The probability of picking one of these blue marbles at random from a bag is $\frac{2}{5}$.

When the probability of an outcome depends on the probability of a previous outcome, it is called **conditional probability**. The conditional probability that the second marble is blue is $\frac{2}{5}$.

Mutually exclusive events
Two or more **events** that cannot both have a **successful outcome** at the same time. For example, if A is the event "choosing a red card from a deck of playing cards" and B is the event "choosing a spade from a deck of playing cards," events A and B are mutually exclusive.

If you pick one playing card from a deck it cannot be a red card and also a spade, so these are mutually exclusive events.

The **total probability** of a complete set of mutually exclusive events always adds up to 1. For example, one set of mutually exclusive events in choosing a card from a deck are:

- choosing a red card ($\frac{26}{52}$)
- choosing a spade ($\frac{13}{52}$)
- choosing a club ($\frac{13}{52}$)

None of these can occur at the same time. If these probabilities are added together:

$$\frac{26}{52} + \frac{13}{52} + \frac{13}{52} = \frac{52}{52} = 1$$

The result is the same if another complete set of mutually exclusive events are added together, such as choosing a black card, choosing a heart and choosing a diamond.

The probability of something not happening is 1 take away the probability that it will happen.

The probability of rolling a die and getting a six is $\frac{1}{6}$.

The probability of rolling a die and getting a number that is not a six (that is, 1, 2, 3, 4, or 5) is $\frac{5}{6}$.

This is equal to $1 - \frac{1}{6}$.

Combining probabilities

The addition rule or or rule

The rule that is used to find the probability* of one of any number of outcomes* occurring. The addition rule states that:

$$P(A \text{ or } B) = P(A) + P(B)$$

where P stands for "the probability of," and A and B are outcomes.

The addition rule can be applied to any number of events, as long as they are mutually exclusive*. For example:

$$P(X \text{ or } Y \text{ or } Z) = P(X) + P(Y) + P(Z)$$

For example, to find the probability of choosing a red card or a spade or the King of Clubs from a deck of playing cards:

$$P(R \text{ or } S \text{ or } KC) = P(R) + P(S) + P(KC)$$

where P stands for "the probability of," R stands for "red," S stands for "spade" and KC stands for "King of Clubs."

There are 52 cards in a deck. 26 of these are red cards, 13 are spades and there is only one King of Clubs so:

$$P(R) = \frac{26}{52}$$
$$P(S) = \frac{13}{52}$$
$$P(KC) = \frac{1}{52}$$
$$P(R \text{ or } S) = \frac{26}{52} + \frac{13}{52} + \frac{1}{52} = \frac{40}{52} = \frac{10}{13}$$

The probability of choosing a red card, a spade, or the King of Clubs is $\frac{10}{13}$.

The addition rule can be used to calculate the probability of choosing either a red card, or a spade, or the King of Clubs.

The multiplication rule or and rule

The rule that is used to find the probability* of a combination of outcomes* occurring. The multiplication rule states that:

$$P(A \text{ and } B) = P(A) \times P(B)$$

where P stands for "the probability of," and A and B are outcomes.

The multiplication rule can be used to find the probability of a combination of independent* or dependent events*.

For example, to find the probability of throwing a 4 with a die and choosing a king from a deck of playing cards, use:

$$P(4 \text{ and } K) = P(4) \times P(K)$$

where P stands for "the probability of," and K stands for "king."

There are 6 numbers on a die and 4 kings in a deck of 52 cards, so:

$$P(4) = \frac{1}{6}$$
$$P(K) = \frac{4}{52}$$
$$P(4 \text{ and } K) = \frac{1}{6} \times \frac{4}{52} = \frac{4}{312} = \frac{1}{78}$$

The probability of throwing a 4 and choosing a king is $\frac{1}{78}$.

To use the multiplication rule to find the probability of a combination of dependent events, first calculate any changes in probability following each outcome, then multiply the results.

For example, to find the probability of choosing a king from a deck of cards and then choosing another king, having not replaced the first, use:

$$P(K \text{ and } K) = P(\text{first } K) \times P(\text{second } K)$$

where P stands for "the probability of," and K stands for "king."

There are 4 kings in a deck of 52 cards, so:

$$P(\text{first } K) = \frac{4}{52}$$
$$P(\text{second } K) = \frac{3}{51}$$
$$P(K \text{ and } K) = \frac{4}{52} \times \frac{3}{51} = \frac{12}{2,652} = \frac{1}{221}$$

The probability of choosing a king from a deck of cards and then choosing another king, having not replaced the first, is $\frac{1}{221}$.

* **Compound event, Dependent events** 113; **Event** 112; **Independent events, Mutually exclusive events** 113;
   Outcome, Probability 112; **Ratio** 24; **Single event** 113.

Possible outcomes

The possible outcomes* of an experiment depend on the number of events* that take place and whether the events are dependent* or independent*.

The possible outcomes of independent events can be recorded in a list.

For example, if a coin is tossed, the possible outcomes can be listed as:

H; T

where H is heads and T is tails.

If two coins are tossed, the number of possible outcomes increases:

HH; HT; TH; TT

And if three coins are tossed, the number of possible outcomes increases again:

HHH; HHT; HTH; HTT; THH; THT; TTH; TTT

Possibility space or probability space

A table that shows the possible outcomes* of a pair of independent events*.

For example, the possibility space below shows the possible outcomes of combined scores from throwing two dice.

		First die				
	1	2	3	4	5	6
1	2	3	4	5	6	7
2	3	4	5	6	7	8
3	4	5	6	7	8	⑨
4	5	6	7	8	⑨	10
5	6	7	8	⑨	10	11
6	7	8	⑨	10	11	12

(Second die)

To find the probability of a certain number being the total score from the two dice, count the number of times that score appears in the table. For example, the number 9 appears four times out of 36 possibilities, so the probability of the total score being 9 is $\frac{4}{36}$, which is $\frac{1}{9}$.

Probability tree diagram

A diagram on which the possible outcomes* of events* are written on the "branches." Probability trees are particularly useful for dependent events*.

For example, if a ball is chosen at random from a bag of 4 red and 5 green balls, the possible outcomes can be shown as:

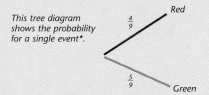

This tree diagram shows the probability for a single event.*

If the first ball is not replaced, and then a second ball is chosen, the probabilities are dependent on the results of the first outcome:

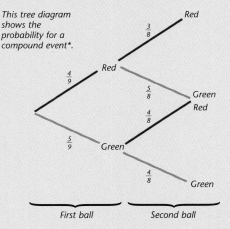

This tree diagram shows the probability for a compound event.*

First ball   Second ball

If a red ball is chosen first, and not replaced, the probability of choosing a second red ball is now only $\frac{3}{8}$ (as only 3 red balls are left out of a total of 8 balls). If a green ball is chosen first, the probability of choosing a second green ball is now only $\frac{4}{8}$ (as only 4 green balls are left out of a total of 8 balls).

Odds

The probability* of an event* occurring expressed as a ratio* of it occurring to it not occurring. For example, the odds of throwing a six with a die are 1:5 (there is one chance of success to five of failure). The probability of throwing a six is $\frac{1}{6}$.

 Internet links For links to useful websites on **probability**, go to *www.usborne-quicklinks.com*

A-Z OF MONEY TERMS

Here is an alphabetical list of some money-related terms you may meet.

Annual percentage rate (APR)
The total cost of any form of borrowing, including **mortgages**, expressed as a percentage* of the amount borrowed. APR includes any administration fees as well as the interest rate*.

Balance
The amount of money in an account when all incomings and outgoings have been considered.

Base rate or **base charges**
A fixed fee charged by a utility company for providing a service to a property. For example, an electricity bill can include a daily base rate plus a cost for each unit of electricity used.

Commission
A fee that is earned for giving a service, such as selling a car on behalf of someone else. Commission is often a percentage* of the value of the item sold.

Credit
Credit has many meanings. In a **credit transaction**, money is received into an account. If your account **has a credit**, it means that you have money. If you **have credit**, you have the ability to borrow money.

Credit balance
The amount of money in your bank account.

Credit card
A card that is used to make purchases but pay for them later. Payments are usually made monthly and interest* may be charged on the amount of money borrowed. A **charge card** or **store card** is a form of credit card issued by a store.

Credit limit
The maximum amount that can be borrowed on a **credit card**.

Credit rating
A points system, based mainly on income and credit history, which is used by banks and other financial institutions to decide how much money a customer can borrow.

Currency
The money in current use by a country. For example, the yen is the currency of Japan.

Debit
Debit has many meanings. In a **debit transaction**, money is taken from an account. If you are **in debit**, you owe money. A **debit** can also mean a sum of money taken from your account.

Debit balance
The amount of money that you owe, for example to a bank or **credit card** company.

Debit card
A card issued by a bank or other financial institution that can be used to make purchases using the money in your bank account.

Deductible
A fixed amount that a person must pay toward an insurance claim. For example, if you have an insurance policy with $100 deductible, you would have to pay the first $100 of any claim, and the insurance company would pay the rest.

Discount
A deduction from the price of an item. A 10% discount means that the price is reduced by 10%.

Earnings
Salary or **wages**. **Gross earnings** is the amount earned before any deductions (such as **income tax**, and **pension** contributions) are made. **Net earnings**, or **take home pay**, is the amount left after deductions have been made.

Exchange rate
The rate at which a unit of one **currency** can be exchanged for another currency.

Income tax
Tax related to a person's **earnings**. Everyone can earn a certain amount without paying tax on it (**personal tax allowance**) and may be able to claim other allowances. Income tax is payable on all earnings above these combined allowances. Tax is charged as a percentage* of **taxable income**: the more you earn, the more tax you pay.

* **Average** 100; **Interest** 28; **Interest rate** 28; **Percentage** 27.

Income tax withholding program
A program by which **income tax** is deducted from a person's **gross earnings**, before any money is paid to the person.

Inflation
An average* increase in the cost of goods and services over time. There are different ways of measuring inflation, such as the Consumer Price Index (**CPI**), which measures the changing cost of a range of commonly used goods and services.

Insurance premium
The amount that you pay to an insurance company. Premiums are usually payable yearly. A **no claims bonus** is a reduction in an insurance premium after several years when no claims have been made.

Investment income
Money received from various forms of investments, such as a **savings account** or **mutual funds**.

Mortgage
A large sum of money loaned by a bank or credit union for buying a house or other property. It is repaid, with interest*, over a number of years.

Overtime
Money paid for working more than the agreed number of hours. Overtime is often paid at a different rate from normal pay.

Pension program
An arrangement to pay a person a regular sum of money after retirement. A pension program is usually funded by payments made before retirement by that person and/or their employer.

Personal loan
A sum of money loaned to a person by a bank for any purpose. The loan is subject to interest*.

Piece rate
A fixed rate of pay that is calculated per item produced or processed, such as the number of bricks laid by a bricklayer. Work that is paid in this way is called **piece-work**.

Salary
The money to be earned over a year. This is usually divided into 12 equal parts, paid monthly.

Sales and services taxes
Taxes that are added to the cost of goods and services, for example, restaurant bills. The amount of tax is a fixed percentage* of the selling price of the goods, and it is decided by the government. Some countries have a combined tax for sales and services called **Value Added Tax** (**VAT**).

Savings account
An account that pays interest* on the money in it.

Statement
A report from a bank or finance company that shows the incomings (amounts received) and outgoings (amounts paid out) of an account. A **credit card** statement will also show how much payment is due.

Stock market
The market for buying and selling stocks and shares in companies. If a company is performing well, its share price is high. If a company is performing poorly, its share price is low.

Tax
Money collected on behalf of the government so they can provide services, such as schools, for the country. There are many different taxes. The act of taxing people is called **taxation**. **Direct taxation** takes place before any money is spent. **Income tax** is a common form of direct taxation. **Indirect taxation** takes place when money is spent. **Sales tax** is an example of indirect taxation.

Unit trust or mutual fund
A program run by an investment company that invests people's money in a range of shares.

Utility bill
A bill for an essential service to a property, such as gas, electricity and water services. Utility bills can be paid weekly, monthly or quarterly.

Wages
The money earned over a period of time, usually paid weekly or monthly after the end of the period.

MATH SYMBOLS

The following list includes symbols commonly used in math that you need to be able to use and recognize. (The letters n and m are used where appropriate to represent any given values.)

$+$ **Addition sign**
(see page 14)
e.g. $2 + 5 = 7$

$-$ **Subtraction sign**
(see page 14)
e.g. $23 - 4 = 19$

$\times$ **Multiplication sign**
(see page 14)
e.g. $6 \times 5 = 30$

$\div$ **Division sign**
(see page 15)
e.g. $45 \div 9 = 5$

$=$ **Equals sign**
(see page 79)
e.g. $2 + 3 = 6 - 1$

n^2 **Squared number**
(see pages 8 and 21)
e.g. $4^2 = 4 \times 4$

n^3 **Cubed number**
(see pages 8 and 21)
e.g. $3^3 = 3 \times 3 \times 3$

$\sqrt{n}$ **Square root**
(see page 11)
e.g. $\sqrt{49} = 7$

$\sqrt[3]{n}$ **Cube root**
(see page 11)
e.g. $\sqrt[3]{125} = 5$

$\%$ **Percent**
(see pages 27–28)
e.g. $\frac{1}{2} = 50\%$

^+n **Positive number**
(see page 7)
e.g. $^+2 \times {^+3} = {^+6}$

^-n **Negative number**
(see page 7)
e.g. $^+3 \times {^-4} = {^-12}$

$\pm n$ **Positive or negative number** (see page 11)
e.g. $\sqrt{16} = \pm 4$

$\overline{n}$ **Recurring number**
(see page 19)
e.g. $10 \div 3 = 3.\dot{3}$

$n{:}m$ **Ratio**
(see pages 24–26)
e.g. $3 : 2$

$\propto$ **Proportional to**
(see pages 25–26)

$n°$ **Degrees**
(see pages 32–33)
e.g. angles in a circle = $360°$

π **Pi** (see page 66)
i.e. $3.141\,592\,654...$

$\angle$ **Angle**
(see page 32–33)
e.g. a right angle is $90°$

$\ulcorner$ **Right angle**
(see page 32)

α **Unknown angle** *alpha*
(see page 60)

θ **Unknown angle** *theta*
(see page 60)

$\equiv$ **Identity sign**
(see page 75)
e.g. $3x \equiv 5x - 2x$

$<$ **Less than**
(see page 90)
e.g. $1 < 3$

$>$ **Greater than**
(see page 90)
e.g. $3 > 1$

$\leqslant$ **Less than or equal to**
(see page 90)

$\geqslant$ **Greater than or equal to**
(see page 90)

$\neq$ **Not equal to**
(see page 90)
e.g. $3 \times 2 \neq 4$

$\approx$ **Is approximately equal to**
(see page 72)
e.g. $100 \div 9 \approx 11$

Σ **The sum of**
(see pages 14 and 101)
e.g. $\Sigma(1, 2, 3) = 6$

$\overline{n}$ **The mean of**
(see page 101)

$\{n\}$ **Set** (see pages 12–13)
e.g. set A = $\{3, 5, 8\}$ and set B = $\{1, 2, 3\}$

$\in$ **Is a member of the set**
(see page 12)
e.g. $3 \in \{3, 5, 8\}$

$\notin$ **Is not a member of the set**
(see page 12)
e.g. $4 \notin \{3, 5, 8\}$

$\mathscr{E}$ **Universal set**
(see page 12)
e.g. $\mathscr{E} = \{\{A\}\{B\}\{...\}\}$

$\varnothing$ or $\{\}$ **Empty set**
(see page 12)

$\cup$ **Union** or **cup**
(see page 13)
e.g. $\{3,5,8\} \cup \{1,2,3\}$
$= \{1, 2, 3, 5, 8\}$

$\cap$ **Intersection** or **cap**
(see page 13)
e.g. $\{3,5,8\} \cap \{1,2,3\}$
$= \{3\}$

INDEX

The page numbers listed in the index are of two types. Those printed in bold type (e.g. **92**) show where the main definitions of words can be found. Page numbers in lighter type (e.g. 92) refer to supplementary entries. Singulars, abbreviations and symbols are given in parentheses after indexed words. If a page number is followed by a word in parentheses, it means that the indexed word can be found inside the text of the definition indicated.

R

radius (*pl.* radii) 51, 57, **65**, 66, 67, 68, 69, 70, 71
random
    events **113**
    sampling **98**
range
    of a distribution **102**, 108, 110
    set of results **92**, 93
rate *see* speed
rates of interest **28** (interest), 29
ratio (*n:m*) **24** (introduction), 25, 26, 52, 66
    method **26**
rational
    number perfect squares **78**
    numbers 9, 12, **78**
raw data **96** (primary data)
real numbers 9, 12, 92
rearranging
    equations 60, 61, 62, **79**, 87, 88, 90
    trigonometric formulas 60, 61, 62, 63
reciprocal **18**, 76, 77
    curve **84**
    functions **93**
    graphs 25, **84**
recording data **99**
rectangles 35, **39**, 56, 67
rectangular coordinate system **31** (Cartesian coordinate system)
rectangular prisms **41**, 58
recurring decimals 9, **19**
reduction 52
reflection **43**, 44
reflection symmetry *or* reflective symmetry **42**
reflex angles **32**, 35
regression line **111**
regular
    polygons 35, 36, 40, 41, 50
    polyhedra **40**, 41
    prisms **41** (prism)
    pyramids **41** (pyramid)
    tessellation 36
relative frequency **112**
remainders (r. *or* rem.) 7, **15**
representing data **105–111**
result (f) **92**
resultant vectors **46**

reverse percentages **27** (to find an original quantity)
revolution **32** (whole turn)
rhombuses 35, **39**
right
    angles 30, **32**, 41, 48, 50, 51, 56, 57, 64, 70, 71
    prisms **41** (prism)
    pyramids **41** (pyramid)
right-angle-hypotenuse-side (RHS) congruence **38**
right-angled triangles **37**, 38, 45, 56, 60–61, 70
roots
    cube **11**, 22
    of quadratic equations **85**
    square **11**, 22, 86
roster notation of sets **12** (set notation)
rotation **43**, 44
rotation symmetry *or* rotational symmetry 39, **42**
round angles *see* whole turns
rounding
    decimals **20**, 86
    error **20**
    integers 9, **16**
rules
    functions 92–93
    in sequences 10
    in sets 12
    of algebra **76–79**

S

salaries **117**
sales and services taxes **117**
samples 97, **98**
sampling **98**
    error **98**
savings accounts **117**
scalar *or* scalar quantity **46**
scalar multiplication **46**
scale **52**
    drawing **52–54**
    factor **44**, 52, 54
scalene triangles **37**
scaling up *or* down **52**
scatter graphs *or* diagrams **110**, 111
scientific notation **21**
secondary data **96**
seconds (s *or* sec) **74**
sectional bar charts **106**

sectors **67**, 68, 105
    area of **67**
segments
    of circles **65**, 70
    of lines **30**, 31, 48, 51
semi-
    circular arcs **65**, 70
    major axes **69** (ellipses)
    minor axes **69** (ellipses)
    regular polyhedra **40**
    regular tessellation **36**
semicircles 51, **65**, 70
sense **43** (reflection)
septagons **34** (polygons)
sequences **10**
sets **12–13**, 92, 98
    notation **12**, 92
shapes *see* polygons
short diagonals **41** (diagonal)
showing proportion **25**
side-angle-side (SAS) congruence **38**
side elevations **41** (elevation)
sides **34**, 35, 37, 49, 60, 62
side-side-side (SSS) congruence **38**
significant figures (sig. fig. *or* s.f.) 6, **9**, 16, 23
similar
    figures **44**
    triangles **38**
simple
    fractions **18**
    interest **28**, 29
    random sampling **98**
simplification
    of expressions and equations **77**, 78, 87, 89
    of fractions *see* canceling fractions
    of ratios **24**
simultaneous equations **87–89**
sine
    graph *or* sine curve 63, **64**
    ratio (sin) **60**, 61, 93
    rule **62**, 63
    wave **64**
single event **113**
size *see* magnitude
slant height **41**, 68
slope (m) 25, **80**, 81
    and tangents **95**
    of graphs 94, 95

upper
    bounds **16**
    class boundaries
        99 (class boundary)
    class limits **99**
        (class interval)
    quartiles (Q_3) **102**,
        109, 110
US customary units **72–73**
utility bills **117**

V

Value Added Tax (VAT)
    117 (sales and services tax)
variables **75, 79, 80, 87,
    88, 90**
variance **103**
variations on graphs **64**, 93
vector notation **45**
vectors 43, **45–46**
velocity **73**, 95
Venn diagrams **13**
vertex *see* vertices

vertical **30**, 31, 50, 95, 106,
    109, 110
vertically opposite angles
    33
vertices (*sing.* vertex) 91
    of polygons 33, **34**, 35, 36,
        37, 48, 57, 70, 71
    of polyhedra **40**, 41
volume **58–59**, 94, 95
    cones **59** (volume of a
        pyramid), **68**
    rectangular prisms **58**
    cylinders **67**
    prisms **58**, 68
    pyramids **59**, 68
    spheres **59, 69**

W

wages **117**
weight **72** (mass)
whiskers **110** (box plot)
whole numbers *see* integers
whole turns **32**, 71

X

x-axis **31** (Cartesian coordinate
    system), 45, 80, 81, 93, 94, 95
x-coordinate **31** (Cartesian
    coordinate system)
x-intercept **80**

Y

yards (yd) **72** (US customary
    units)
y-axis **31** (Cartesian
    coordinate system), 45, 80,
    81, 93, 94, 95
y-coordinate **31** (Cartesian
    coordinate system)
y-intercept **80**, 81

Z

z-axis **31** (dimensions)
zero
    angles **32**
    exponent rule **22**
zig-zags **110**

Acknowledgements

Website adviser
Lisa Watts

Photos
Page 23 ©UC Regents/Lick Observatory; page 35 courtesy of GlobeXplorer.*

*Every effort has been made to trace the copyright holders of the material in this book. If any rights have been omitted, the publishers offer to rectify this in any future edition, following notification. The publishers are grateful to the organizations and individuals concerned for their contribution and permission to reproduce material.

Trademarks
Macintosh and QuickTime are trademarks of Apple Computer, Inc., registered in the US and other countries.
RealOne Player is a trademark or registered trademark of RealNetworks, Inc., registered in the US and other countries.
Flash and Shockwave are trademarks of Macromedia, Inc., registered in the US and other countries.

Usborne Publishing is not responsible and does not accept liability for the availability or content of any website other than its own, or for any exposure to harmful, offensive, or inaccurate material which may appear on the Web. Usborne Publishing will have no liability for any damage or loss caused by viruses that may be downloaded as a result of browsing the sites it recommends.

First published in 2003 by Usborne Publishing Ltd,
Usborne House, 83-85 Saffron Hill, London EC1N 8RT, England.
AE First published in America, 2004.
www.usborne.com

Printed in Italy.

EDC 10/04 20.95